STRESS SCRIPTING

STRESS SCRIPTING

A
GUIDE TO
STRESS MANAGEMENT

Jonathan C. Smith

1991

New York
Westport, Connecticut
London

Library of Congress Cataloging-in-Publication Data

Smith, Jonathan C.
    Stress scripting : a guide to stress management / Jonathan C.
Smith.
        p.   cm.
    Includes bibliographical references and index.
    ISBN 0-275-93639-2 (alk. paper)
    1. Stress management.   I. Title.
RA785.S66   1991
155.9'042—dc20   90-38840

British Library Cataloguing in Publication Data is available.

Library of Congress Catalog Card Number: 90-38840
ISBN: 0-275-93639-2

First published in 1991

Praeger Publishers, One Madison Avenue, New York, NY 10010
An imprint of Greenwood Publishing Group, Inc.

Printed in the United States of America

The paper used in this book complies with the
Permanent Paper Standard issued by the National
Information Standards Organization (Z39.48-1984).

10 9 8 7 6 5 4 3 2 1

To
Miriam Ben-Shalom, Robert Bettiker,
David Carney, James Holobaugh,
Joseph Steffan, and Leonard Mattlovich

Contents

PART 3: A RELAXATION SUPPLEMENT

PART 4: EXERCISES

Preface:
A Message for
Therapists and Instructors

This book begins with a simple assertion: We are all stress experts. Stress can be a problem almost anywhere--in therapy, business, school, the hospital recovery room, or even church. It should be no surprise that the tools of stress management have exceptionally broad applicability. We focus on three: assertiveness training, cognitive restructuring, and relaxation. Our guiding, cognitive-behavioral perspective is that good stress management is based on sensible problem-solving.

I have designed *Stress Scripting* to be a versatile stress management tool. It is a book I use in therapy, workshops, university instruction, and consultation to business. As a supplement to therapy, *Stress Scripting* can be presented to clients as outside reading. Individual treatment can be augmented with weekly stress scripting groups, freeing up valuable therapy time for more difficult issues.

In addition, *Stress Scripting* can be a helpful resource for a variety of workshops and seminars. With small modifications, individual chapters can be selected and used for programs on assertiveness, cognitive restructuring, burnout, job stress, supervision, problem solving, pain management, relapse prevention, anger management, relaxation, negotiation, and so on. Similarly, *Stress Scripting* can serve as a primary or supplementary text for undergraduate courses in stress management, health psychology, behavioral medicine, adjustment, and even introductory psychology.

Finally, health professionals are becoming increasingly involved as stress consultants for business. *Stress Scripting* can serve as the foundation for a variety of training programs. In addition, since the scripting approach is designed to require minimal professional supervision, groups can be facilitated by in-house staff. This can be a highly cost-effective strategy for introducing stress management, and provide the foundation for a variety of other, more individualized programs.

HOW THIS BOOK IS ORGANIZED

Stress Scripting consists of four parts.   Chapters can be used together or, with minor revisions, separately. Part 1 presents the basic ideas of stress management defense and coping, assertiveness, thinking and stress, cues, reinforcement, and the phases of stress. The overall objective is didactic, to let the client know what stress and stress management are.   Part 1 concludes with an option to contract for behavior change. Therapists may wonder why we do not begin *Stress Scripting* with contracted behavior change assignments. Although this indeed can be done, I have found it more useful to first thoroughly explain what stress management is. I believe clients should know what they are getting into before formally committing to change.

Part 2 is a bit more challenging and concentrates on behavior change. We consider assertiveness scripts, relapse prevention, problem solving and negotiation, desensitization, and the coping philosophy. Each chapter contains its own behavioral objectives.   Once again, a therapist may chose to use all or some of Part 2.   Some may find it useful to begin Part 2 with Chapter 11, which outlines a variation of stress inoculation training that can be applied to every chapter in Part 2.

This book will work best if clients have already mastered, or are in the process of mastering, a relaxation technique. Indeed, by the time clients begin Part 2, it is assumed they already know something about relaxation.   Mental health professionals often prefer vastly differing approaches, ranging from hypnosis and biofeedback to progressive relaxation and meditation. So many techniques are available, each with differing effects, that it is a good idea to experiment with several.

Rather than impose yet another relaxation system, *Stress Scripting* can be integrated with whatever approach the user prefers.   For supplementary purposes, Part 3 presents an abbreviated relaxation training program based on cognitive-behavioral relaxation theory (Smith, 1989, 1990). This can be incorporated into Parts 1 and 2. The user may also choose to complete *Relaxation Dynamics* (Smith, 1989), a comprehensive self-help program coordinated with *Stress Scripting*. For advice on teaching relaxation, health professionals are advised to consult Smith (1990).

Stress Scripting concludes in Part 4 with a series of exercises. Some can be completed individually, whereas others are for stress-management groups. In addition, most individual exercises can be easily modified for group use. Exercises for Chapters 6-12 are preceded by a contract in which the client indicates willingness to attempt behavior change, and how he or she will be rewarded upon completion. Such contracts can increase the effectiveness of self-help programs.

INNOVATIONS IN *STRESS SCRIPTING*

Bookstores are filled with stress management books. *Stress Scripting* is different. It is designed to be an accessible self-help guide that does not sacrifice scholarship. It is a book for therapists and instructors as well as clients and students.

Stress Scripting focuses on general and practical stress management. To maximize versatility, a number of limited-domain areas of theory and research often found in stress management books have been omitted. These include life change events, Type A behavior, personality and stress, physiological stress mechanisms, the immune system, and various aspects of job stress. I believe that the tools presented in *Stress Scripting* are truly general and can be applied to many specific areas of concern. For example, a stress management group may include a Type A business executive, someone dealing with life change events, and a cancer patient worried about the link between stress and health. The Type A individual may have little interest in cancer, life change events, and so on. Similarly, clients dealing with cancer or life change may not want to hear about Type A behavior. However, all may well benefit from relaxation, assertiveness training, and cognitive restructuring. The general and applied approach of *Stress Scripting* enables the therapist or instructor to supplement stress management with an introduction to whatever domains of theory and research are deemed appropriate.

In addition, some minor and somewhat technical innovations are worth noting. Chapter 3 summarizes the results of over 20 factor analytic studies of assertiveness inventories, and clearly explains the link between assertiveness, defense, and coping. Chapter 5 simplifies key cognitive-behavioral constructs by integrating the temporal components of stress inoculation training (pre-stress, mid-stress, and post-stress) with the notion of stimulus cues and reinforcement. Chapter 8 emphasizes the conceptual similarity of problem solving and negotiation. Chapters 9 and 10 focus on relapse prevention, an important idea frequently avoided in stress management books. In addition, Chapter 10 introduces a new way of interrelating and conceptualizing pain management and burnout in terms of relapse prevention. Chapter 12 concludes with a discussion of "coping philosophies," an innovation in cognitive-behavioral treatment that represents a step beyond cognitive restructuring irrational or maladaptive assumptions and beliefs. Finally, *Stress Scripting* is currently the only stress management book that incorporates cognitive-behavioral relaxation training (Smith, 1990).

Part 1

Basic Stress Scripting

1

Getting Started

We are all stress experts. Nearly everyone can recall an illness aggravated by pressure, a mistake caused by preoccupation with worry, or any of a large number of symptoms associated with stress. For over a decade, the popular press has heightened our awareness of such problems. Stress is a major contributor to heart disease, cancer, respiratory illness, insomnia, and ulcers. Stress plays an important part in alcohol and drug abuse, smoking, and obesity. And stress contributes to accident-proneness, lowered efficiency and creativity. Stress is indeed costly. Its annual price tag to business has been estimated at $150 billion each year (Murphy and Schoenborn, 1987).

What many people do not realize is that much stress can be prevented. In fact, stress management is something of a boom industry. The reason is clear. Carol Schneider, past president of the American Biofeedback Society, has estimated that businesses can save an average of five dollars for every dollar spent on stress management (Schneider, 1987). Stress management may well be good business; however, it is also expensive business. Quality programs can cost hundreds or thousands of dollars. There has to be a better, less expensive way.

For years I have felt the need for good, inexpensive stress management. I did nothing until a local television station invited me to appear on a special program about stress. Feeling a little jittery, I decided to go to one of the largest bookstores in Chicago and check the state of the stress management business. Here was my strategy: count all the books listed under stress. One hour turned into two. Eventually, I spent the entire day wandering up and down aisles counting books. (The bookstore manager was beginning to worry about this strange behavior.) The total astounded me: 71 books on stress (for comparison, I counted only 70 on dieting).

Once I started examining these books, a serious problem became apparent. Some were rather stodgy textbooks filled with facts and theories. These were hardly appropriate for helping one actually deal more effectively with stress. Others carefully outlined the causes and costs of stress. In a rapidly developing field, these books were often out of date as soon as they were published. Still others offered only one or two stress management techniques, ignoring important approaches accepted by psychologists. In sum, not a single book could honestly claim to be a thorough, usable guide to stress management. At this point I decided, with some trepidation, to write my own.

This book contains the ideas and exercises I have found most useful in helping others deal with stress. Using a practical, problem-solving approach we consider the basics of interpersonal stress, stress-producing thoughts and worries, and relaxation. Then we move on to advanced stress management. I have used this book, both in its entirety and selected chapters, in a wide range of settings. Many clients find the entire book a useful supplement to therapy. Chapters can be presented as stress workshops or as tools for orienting clients to therapy. The book is appropriate for self-led groups on stress management as well as university stress courses.

STRESS SCRIPTS

In his play, *As You Like It*, Shakespeare wrote that we are but actors on a stage. If the stresses of life can be seen as a play, we often write and act our own scripts. This is the idea underlying *Stress Scripting*. It is not new--you already use it. Let me give you an example.

Martin is manager for a small real estate business. His doctor has explained that his high blood pressure is probably stress related. One look at how Martin deals with the problems in living reveals why. For example, last month he hired Sue as a sales representative. Sue was fairly new to the real estate business and was making a few beginner's errors. Most irritating to Martin was her tendency not to take phone messages while he was away. This happened twice. Each time, Martin ignored the problem, assuming Sue would do better. When Sue failed to note her third message, he exploded:

"Why aren't you doing your job? Do you think I have to do everything around here? Unless you get over your laziness, you'll never get anywhere in this office."

That night, Martin was upset about his encounter. He realized that his emotional explosion was probably not very helpful to Sue, and that perhaps he should have said:

"Sue, because this business is small, we should all take messages for each other when needed. This is very important, because if a message isn't taken down, we might lose a valuable customer. And when that happens, we all lose."

It might surprise you to hear that Martin already knows how to manage stress. His only problem is that he figures out how to cope after the fact. How many times has this happened to you? Have you ever muddled through a stress situation only to realize, after things are over, what you could have said or done? Stress hindsight is often 20/20. However, it is not my goal to make you feel guilty about coming up with answers too late, but to show that you may already possess some skill at stress scripting.

Whenever you think back and mentally redo a stress situation, you are writing a script. The problem, of course, is that your script is a little late. The stress scripting approach is very simple--you plan ahead of time what you are going to think and do, and then practice until your script becomes automatic. The idea is to make your stress scripts so habitual that eventually you will not have think about what to do or say, just as an expert actor can say his or her lines naturally, almost as if the play were happening in real life.

THE TEST

We are now ready to get to work. Is stress a problem for you? What kinds of stress are most serious in your life? To answer these questions we need to take a look at what stress is. The first answers many people give go something like this:

"Stress is getting a headache."
"Stress is worrying about my children."
"Stress is feeling uptight and cynical at work."
"Stress is just feeling tired."

These answers reveal one thing most of us know about stress--it is an unpleasant, unwanted experience. When we are upset, hurt, or tense, we are stressed. This is a useful place to begin. Feelings of distress motivate us to take action, and hopefully learn more powerful coping skills. They can serve as early warning signals, cues to take action and use our coping skills.

There are actually three general categories of distress: unwanted and uncontrollable thought or worry, negative emotion, and physical symptoms. Some people react to stress with worry. They are likely to describe their distress this way:

"Negative thoughts go through my mind."
"I can't seem to control my worry."

Others are more likely to experience a variety of stressful emotions. Some of the more basic ones (Izard, 1977) include:

"I feel anxious."
"I am depressed."
"I am angry."
"I feel afraid."

However, physical symptoms are perhaps the most common sign of stress. Many symptoms are signs of the body's emergency flight or fight reaction. You may already know that each of us has a built-in stress energy response (the "adrenalin rush," although this notion is a bit oversimplified). When triggered by stress, the brain automatically sends signals throughout the body to prepare it for vigorous action. Heart and breathing rate quickens, muscles tighten, brain activity increases--all to prepare to fight or flee. This reaction is absolutely essential for survival. It is what gives the football player the quick shot of energy when catching the ball. The stress response enables you to defend yourself when attacked by a dog in the street.

However, there is a problem. The flight or fight response can also be triggered by simple worry and everyday hassles--the alarm clock, getting stuck in a traffic jam, dealing with a critical client or boss, wondering if you have enough time to finish a critical report, feeling down about yourself, and so on. In fact, many of us experience such high levels of chronic stress that we simply get used to it. But stress still takes its silent toll on our bodies. The heart, digestive system, and lungs are subjected to wear and tear and resistance to disease is lowered. We become more vulnerable to a wide range of illnesses.

Fortunately, our bodies often tell us when stress is building before it is too late. Some symptoms directly indicate the energy response. For example:

Rapid, irregular pounding heart
Breathing difficulties
Restlessness
Tense muscles

Some are less direct signs of wear and tear:

Perspiring
Feeling too warm
Dry mouth

And some are aftereffects of continued wear and tear:

Fatigue
Headaches
Backaches

Here is the complete Stress TEST (which stands for stress Thinking Emotions Symptoms Test). If you are interested in taking it complete Exercise 1.1 in Part 4.

The Stress TEST

Thought and Worry

___ 1. I worry too much about things that do not really matter.
___ 2. I have difficulty keeping troublesome thoughts out of my mind.
___ 3. Anxiety-provoking thoughts run through my mind.
___ 4. Unimportant thoughts run through my mind and bother me.
___ 5. I worry about things even when I know worrying is not making anything better.
___ 6. I find it difficult to control negative thoughts.

Negative Emotion

___ 7. I feel distressed (discouraged, downhearted, or sad).
___ 8. I feel irritated or angry (annoyed, provoked, mad, or defiant).
___ 9. I feel contempt.
___ 10. I feel distaste or disgust.

___ 11. I feel shy or sheepish.
___ 12. I feel fearful.
___ 13. I feel depressed.
___ 14. I feel anxious.

Physical Symptoms

___ 15. My heart beats fast, hard, or irregularly.
___ 16. My breathing feels hurried, shallow, or uneven.
___ 17. My muscles feel tight, tense, or clenched up (furrowed brow, making fist, clenching jaws, etc.).
___ 18. I feel restless and fidgety (tapping fingers or feet, fingering things, pacing, shifting in seat, chewing or biting, blinking, etc.).
___ 19. I feel tense or self-conscious when I say or do something.
___ 20. I perspire too much or feel too warm.
___ 21. I feel the need to go to the rest room even when I do not have to.
___ 22. I feel uncoordinated.
___ 23. My mouth feels dry.
___ 24. I feel tired, fatigued, worn out, or exhausted.
___ 25. I have a headache.
___ 26. I feel unfit or heavy.
___ 27. My back aches.
___ 28. My shoulders, neck, or back feels tense.
___ 29. The condition of my skin seems worse (blemishes, too oily).
___ 30. My eyes are watering or teary.
___ 31. My stomach is nervous and uncomfortable.
___ 32. I have lost my appetite.

Distressing behavior, speech, thought, emotion, and symptoms do not just happen. In lessons to come we will discover some of their underlying causes, and what we can do to cope more effectively.

2

Basic Stress Scripts

One of the difficulties people have with stress is not seeing connections. We tend to remember highlights (the screaming child, slammed door, or upset stomach) or vague general impressions (feeling upset or frustrated, etc.). The same is true with watching a movie where, a month later, you might recall only the stirring finish or that it was somehow a "thrilling movie." Yet, like a movie plot, an entire stress situation is a chain of specific interconnected events.

Every movie, to continue with our analogy, is based on a script that tells the actors what to say and do. In addition, a script provides useful information to the actors about what the characters are thinking and feeling. There are good and bad scripts, and the difference can help us understand stress better. To explore this idea, we will begin with the imaginary tale of Mollie McPhareland.

Mollie was a famous actress, noted particularly for her portrayals of hassled housewives in soap operas. One day she was handed a script for a new program, "Gretchen and the Boss." She glanced at it briefly, gasped, and tossed it away exclaiming, "I simply can't do this. This is just impossible!" And she walked off the set. Soon Mollie McPhareland was front page news. Rumors abounded about possible indecencies written into the script, or perhaps a part that reminded her of some secret childhood trauma. We can now share with you part of the notorious script. In this section Gretchen, a new secretary, has an encounter with her boss. See if you can figure out why Mollie called this script "impossible."

GRETCHEN: Storms into the office.
BOSS: Gets steamed up.
GRETCHEN: Blows up and creates a scene.
BOSS: Acts like a pig.
GRETCHEN: Throws in the towel.

This is a strange script indeed. Notice there are no specific words for any of the characters to say. Instead, the only thing presented are vague generalizations ("storms into office," "gets steamed up," "blows up," "acts like pig," and "throws in the towel"). Mollie simply did not know what she was supposed to say or do. And very little was given about her feelings and interpretations. Here is a revised script that presents this crucial information more clearly:

GRETCHEN: (Walks into office and slams door. Faces her boss, trying to make her problem perfectly clear.) "Yesterday you gave me three extra papers to do, and no extra time. "
BOSS: (Getting angry since this is the third complaint he's heard today.) "Your work is always substandard. I think you should make serious efforts to improve."
GRETCHEN: (Her hands start to tremble. She feels attacked and thinks the boss is accusing her of being a lazy bum.) "This is unfair. I am getting very frustrated and angry working here. Each day you have given me three or four extra papers to do. And now this."
BOSS: (Feeling angry because Gretchen is not dealing with the problem. He sighs, looks to the ceiling, and with some sarcasm, blurts out a cutting comment.) "I should have hired a male. You women are all alike."
GRETCHEN: (Shocked and angered by this sexist comment, makes a fist.) "I simply cannot work under these conditions. I quit."

A script like this tells you exactly what is happening. In describing your stress situations, this is what to strive for. Present just the facts: what was said and done, and what you thought and felt. Put simply, *write your script so it could be acted by someone else.*

Now let us examine another example. Lance has a poor understanding of his stress. Here is his description of what is going on. Can you see why he might have some trouble learning to cope with this situation more effectively?

"Whenever I ask my roommate to carry his weight, he just acts like a bum."

If we look at this account closely, it really tells us very little, except that Lance is upset. We know nothing about what he or his roommate actually said or did. If you wanted to give Lance some advice, you wouldn't know where to begin. Indeed, he probably wouldn't know what kind of advice to ask for. See if you can tell how the following account provides much more useful information.

Last week I asked my roommate to help clean the apartment. My request was simple: "Laundry and newspapers are littered all over the rug. I can't even find a place to stand. This makes me feel very frustrated, like you don't care about the place." He answered "I will clean up in due time." I thought, "Here we go again. This is the same excuse he gave last week." Getting a bit irritated, I specifically asked, "I would like you to help clean for one hour tonight. That way we can begin to get this place straightened out." He said he would think about it and walked out.

We know exactly what happened, the concrete behaviors and speech of each person. In addition, we know the one roommate feels frustrated and irritated. This is much more specific, and revealing than saying that the roommate "ignores and upsets me." And since we know the specifics, we can begin to think about what needs to be done to resolve this situation.

BASIC STRESS SCRIPTS

Imagine you are creating a script that describes a recent stressful situation. Writing a script so that someone else might act it out can help you remember details and be more objective. It is as if you are replaying a movie in slow motion so you can see important details you may have missed. Any script has four possible types of lines:

Behavior Lines describe actions (i.e., postures, facial expressions, movements, and what is done with the hands and feet).
Speech Lines present what is actually said.
Feeling Lines describe emotions (distress, irritation, anger, distaste, shyness, fear, depression, anxiety, etc.) and physical symptoms (headache, backache, stomach problems, feeling warm, fatigue,

etc.) such as those that appear on the Stress TEST.

Thought Lines present thoughts and ideas. They describe what is going on in one's mind as well as any recognized reasons for behaviors, speech, negative emotion, and physical symptoms.

There's one simple rule for writing stress scripts. When you are describing a person other than yourself, present only their Behavior and Speech Lines. Why? Because you can not see their thoughts and feelings--these are personal, hidden events. However, for yourself describe everything, Thought and Feeling as well as Behavior and Speech Lines.

Now we are ready for an example.

GENERAL SITUATION: Asking a friend to return a borrowed book.
YOU

BEHAVIOR LINE: My friend is sitting at a table in the cafeteria. I walk up to him and sit down.
SPEECH LINE: "John, last month I lent you my book of poems. I wonder if you still have it."
FEELING LINE: I feel tense, and my stomach is getting uneasy.
THOUGHT LINE: "I really want my book back. I will be firm about this goal. However, I wonder if my friend remembers borrowing my book. How should I bring up the topic without embarrassing him?"

OTHER PERSON: MY FRIEND

BEHAVIOR LINE: Sits up in his chair, turns to me, and looks confused.
SPEECH LINE: "I'm sorry. I thought I returned your book last week. Let me check when I get home."

YOU

BEHAVIOR LINE: I lean back, and look him straight in the eye.
SPEECH LINE: "I'm sure it was just an oversight on your part. But I would like to have the book back. Could you return it by Friday?"
FEELING LINE: Tension is reduced.
THOUGHT LINE: "He sounds sincere. I hope he means it. I don't think it would be inappropriate for me to frankly ask for the book"

THOUGHT LINES: A SPECIAL PROBLEM

Imagine you are watching a mystery movie. A housewife takes a walk alone through the park late at night. Suddenly she hears heavy footsteps behind her. In the movie, the housewife says nothing--she does not want to give herself away. However, the director lets you know what is going on in her mind. From the screen, we hear her thinking, "What's that! I hope I'm not being followed!"

In a movie, the director often lets you know what actors are thinking. You hear their inner dialogues, even though they actually may be completely silent. Such silent dialogues include thoughts ("I wonder what I should do next; I hope I'm doing the right thing"). These go in your Thought Lines. The director may also tell you what a character is feeling ("Boy, my back aches. I feel anxious. This is making me sad"). These are not thoughts, but emotions and symptoms that go in the Feeling Lines.

Thought Lines are often the most important part of a script. However, they can cause special problems for script writers. In the fleeting moment of a stress situation it can be difficult to remember what went through your mind. You might wonder, "I wasn't thinking anything. I just acted." If you are having difficulty, put down what you probably would have thought. You might think of a cartoon of yourself, with a "thought balloon" over your head. What words would you put in your thought balloon? Another strategy is to imagine what someone else who is just like you would have thought. Or, look at your Behavior, Feeling, and Speech Lines and ask the question: "Why did I behave (feel or speak) in the way described?" Your answer to this question can reveal what was going on in your mind at the time. Remember, your Thought Lines do not have to be perfect. An approximation of what went through your mind is good enough.

It can be useful to note that overall goals and evaluations are usually presented in Thought Lines ("I really want my book back. I will be firm about this goal"). You might find this a bit confusing and, by mistake, put your goals and evaluations in your Behavior Lines. The reason why they belong in Thought Lines is that they represent what is going on in your mind. This becomes more clear in the following script:

GENERAL SITUATION: Saying no to a coworker's insistent requests to write his report for him.

OTHER PERSON: COWORKER

BEHAVIOR LINE: Looks at me very sincerely. Looks very sad.
SPEECH LINE: "I wonder if you could help me out and write this report for me."

YOU

BEHAVIOR LINE: Sit facing coworker.
SPEECH LINE: "Can't you find someone else to help?"
FEELING LINE: Irritation.
THOUGHT LINE: "Here we go again. I almost feel like he's trying to take advantage of me. I really object to this behavior."

OTHER PERSON: COWORKER

BEHAVIOR LINE: Continues looking at me sincerely and sadly.
SPEECH LINE: "Oh, come on. Please help me. You've been so good to me in the past."

YOU

BEHAVIOR LINE: Sit facing coworker.
SPEECH LINE: "I just can't help you. I'm sorry."
FEELING LINE: Irritation, stomach trouble.
THOUGHT LINE: "I've just about had it. This is as bad as he's ever been. I just won't do it."

Notice the judgments and interpretations ("I really object . . . This is as bad as he's ever been.") appear as Thought Lines. In addition, notice that in this example Behavior Lines do not change. In every case, you "sit facing coworker" and the coworker "looks sincerely and sadly." Often lines have to be repeated. This simply indicates that what is important is taking place on another line.

To give you some practice in scripting, here is another script. Take a look at how the person described is responding to the situation. Think about what your Thought, Feeling, Behavior, and Speech Lines might be.

GENERAL SITUATION: Protesting to a police office about a parking ticket.

OTHER PERSON: POLICE OFFICER

BEHAVIOR LINE: Approaches as you are entering your car.

SPEECH LINE: "Excuse me, but this is not a legal parking place. You have parked in a bus stop. I'm sorry, but I will have to give you a ticket."

YOU

BEHAVIOR LINE: Look confused. Shake head back and forth. Scratch head. Open car door and exit. Stand next to police, looking to one side.

SPEECH LINE: "I'm very sorry, officer. I just didn't notice. I was getting ready to move my car away. It won't happen again."

FEELING LINE: Guilt, anxiety, tense shoulders.

THOUGHT LINE: "Oh no! He's caught me. I've done something terribly wrong. How could I be so stupid?"

THE SERGEANT FRIDAY *SCRIPT* RULES

We have now completed the basics of stress scripting. At this time it might be useful to stand back and take a more general look at what makes an effective script. Good scripts follow what I like to call the Sergeant Friday SCRIPT Rule. You may recall the popular television show, Dragnet, starring Sergeant Joe Friday. One of the program's comical (and somewhat sexist) trademarks was the "rambling witness scene." Here, Friday would patiently listen to a seemingly endless list of irrelevant details, pointless opinions, emotional outbursts, or uncalled-for interpretations. Finally, he would interrupt with the curt request, "Just the facts, ma'am. Just the facts." And that is what makes an effective stress script. Specifically, it should be Simple, Concrete, Realistic, Important, Personal, and Timely (notice that the first letters of these words spell "SCRIPT"--a useful memory cue):

Simple. Does your script focus on one or two things rather than an entire "laundry list"?

Concrete. Does your script focus on concrete, observable behaviors and events? Does it indicate who, when, what, and where? Do you avoid the use of psychoanalyzing, or of vague and abstract terms, emotional outbursts, name-calling, or overstating?

Realistic. Is your script realistic or unattainable and excessive? Have you included the facts of the situation, rather than guesses, innuendos, rumors, and so on?

Important. Have you identified what is truly important to you? Have you focused on the real problem, rather than just the symptom. Have you identified the cause, rather than a relatively unimportant effect?

Personal. Is it significant to you?

Timely. Does your script focus on what is relatively recent and fresh, rather than history and "water under the bridge"?

THE VALUE OF STRESS SCRIPTING

How does scripting help us deal with stress? First, it counters our tendency to think of stress in vague, global, and emotional terms. It is often considerably more useful to deal with a specific, identifiable situation ("It wears me out having to supervise 25 clients; my job description calls for 10 clients") rather than global impressions ("Work is just too much for me"). Scripting also forces us to divide a stressful encounter into meaningful and specific "chunks." Doing this can put things in a new light and contribute to new approaches to coping. To see how this can happen, let us examine the following examples.

Jill is upset with her husband, Bill. She feels that all of the household chores end up on her lap and wishes Bill would take on more responsibility. Before writing a stress script, she might describe her stress situation in the following way:

"Bill's just too irresponsible. I'm always doing all the work around the house. I'm getting fed up with his laziness. He doesn't care about me."

However, things appeared a bit differently after Jill produced the following stress script.

GENERAL SITUATION: Asking Bill to help in the garden.

JILL

BEHAVIOR LINE: Sits next to Bill. Looks into air.
SPEECH LINE: "Bill, the garden really needs work. We must plant the tulips before it's too late. And weeds are beginning to take over."
FEELING LINE: Urgent anticipation
THOUGHT LINE: "I really want him to help. The garden belongs to both of us. Its only fair that he do some of the work."

BILL

BEHAVIOR LINE: Gets up from sofa. Begins to walk out of the room to the kitchen.
SPEECH LINE: "Not now, honey. Maybe some other day."

JILL

BEHAVIOR LINE: Walks with Bill to kitchen.
SPEECH LINE: "Bill, I'm getting really frustrated. I've made what seems like a reasonable request, to help in our garden, and you don't even express a willingness to help. I just don't know what to make of your lack of interest. I wonder if you don't care about the work I have to do."
FEELING LINE: Frustration and irritation
THOUGHT LINE: "Why won't he help me? This isn't fair. Doesn't he care about all the work I have to do? Is he just being selfish?"

After writing this script, Jill could see her stress situation a bit more clearly. Her first reaction ("Bill's just too irresponsible . . . I'm getting fed up with his laziness. He doesn't care about me") is not really the problem. Indeed, looking at the script, we can see that her first reaction was far too vague, emotional, and overblown. The script pinpoints a specific, concrete problem: helping out in the garden. It also makes clear a coping option, simply telling Bill what is going on.

Here is another situation that illustrates a different problem. George has a small mole on his right hand. He realizes it might require minor surgery. To find out, he has scheduled a visit with his doctor. For a week prior to the visit he has been considerably upset about his problem. Here's how he first describes it: "This surgery has really done a number on me. I'm just a mental case. I don't think I can take it." However, after writing a script, we can understand George's problem better:

GENERAL SITUATION: Talking to a friend about the upcoming doctor's visit.

GEORGE

BEHAVIOR LINE: Walking to work with friend. Both stop, and I turn to my friend to say something.

SPEECH LINE: "I'm really upset about seeing my doctor. God, what if I have to have surgery? This upsets me."

FEELING LINE: Panic and anxiety

THOUGHT LINE: "What if my doctor says I must have surgery. I bet it's really going to hurt. I just can't stand pain. This is just going to be the end of the world. Why do such awful things have to happen to me."

George's Thought Line reveals something very interesting. He appears to be catastrophizing, making a mountain out of a molehill. Sure, the operation may hurt. But he will survive. It hardly deserves being called "the end of the world." It is clear that one major source of George's panic and anxiety are his exaggerated thoughts.

This final situation is a bit different. Marjorie is a secretary at a local school. She complains that her job is "getting to me." Frequently, she experiences anxiety. As Marjorie puts it, "This job is just too much. I get so anxious that I don't know what to do." Clearly, this is a rather vague description of a stress situation. The following script helps clarify matters.

GENERAL SITUATION: Getting anxious at work.

MARJORIE

BEHAVIOR LINE: Calmly types away.

SPEECH LINE: Says nothing.

FEELING LINE: Interest

THOUGHT LINE: "This test I'm working on is longer than usual. No problem. I'll get it done."

PROFESSOR JONES

BEHAVIOR LINE: Walks into the office unannounced to get a cup of coffee. Looks at Marjorie without saying a thing.

MARJORIE

BEHAVIOR LINE: Continues typing. Looks up and notices Professor Jones. Makes a few mistakes typing.

SPEECH LINE: Says nothing.

FEELING LINE: Anxiety and panic

THOUGHT LINE: "Oh no, that creep again. I don't like Professor Jones. He never talks to me. Why is he looking at me? This is bad. I'm getting anxious again. I'm making so many mistakes. I can't type. Professor Jones is staring at me. I bet he can tell exactly how anxious I am. He must think I'm really nuts."

As was the case with George, Marjorie also creates stress for herself through her Thought Lines. But something else is going on. Marjorie's anxiety is not constant. Sometimes she feels it and sometimes she does not. In fact, we can identify a clear anxiety trigger: Professor Jones walking into the office and staring at her. Before this cue, Marjorie was doing fine.

The three scripts we have considered illustrate the importance of taking an objective, problem-solving approach to understanding stress. Instead of reacting to stress in a vague, global, and emotional manner, we must break it down into component events. The scripts also reveal three important dimensions of stress. First, stress is often increased or reduced by the degree to which we directly and assertively express our thoughts and feelings. In addition, our thoughts play an important role in creating and aggravating stress. Finally, to understand stress completely, we need to understand how it is timed, the cues that tell us when stress is beginning and ending. In the following chapters we will consider more thoroughly assertiveness, thought stress, and stress cues.

3

Coping, Defense, and People Stress

There are two general ways of dealing with stress--coping and defense. When we cope, we actively make attempts to change things. However, sometimes coping is not possible, effective, or readily available and the best we can expect is to protect ourselves by reducing the costs, pain, or discomfort of stress. All of us use such defensive strategies: for example, yelling to blow off steam, walking away from a crisis for "time off," crying on a friend's shoulder, or simply reading a book for relaxation. Some defensive strategies are useful, whereas others can be self-destructive. We first consider self-destructive strategies.

SELF-DESTRUCTIVE DEFENSE

Children can give us the clearest examples of self-destructive defensive behavior, and my ten-year old nephew Ronnie is no exception. Like most children, Ronnie can get quite upset when things do not go his way. One day he wanted to buy a new bike. His parents felt he was not ready and objected. First, Ronnie tried a coping strategy-- reasoning. He carefully explained, "All my friends have bikes. I'll be very careful with it." His parents still objected, arguing that he already had a bike and didn't need another. Finally, Ronnie quit being reasonable and simply went to his room. He would not come to dinner. He would not talk to anyone. He was avoiding the problem altogether.

Avoidance is a global defensive strategy we all learn in childhood. When we feel that all attempts at coping have failed, its easy to simply withdraw. Maybe the problem will go away on its own. At least, if we don't have to confront the problem, we can pretend it isn't there. Avoidance is a strategy many adults use. It can be self-destructive, for example, when one runs from difficulties through alcohol and drugs. Simply staying home from work, or taking longer and longer coffee breaks, is another type of avoidance. Perhaps the most subtle avoidance strategy is emotional avoidance, simply withdrawing emotionally from a problem. For example, the frustrated teacher deals with parent complaints by pulling back from work and not investing interest and energy in what she is doing.

My nephew Ronnie has on occasion shown another defensive strategy, the opposite of avoidance. Homework is a problem in my sister's household. Nobody wants to do it. At one point Ronnie's parents decided to get tough and demand he do at least an hour's worth of homework every night. He rebelled, screaming and complaining. He even kicked the poor dog. Ronnie was using attack as a defensive strategy. Although adults rarely display temper tantrums, they often resort to equally self-destructive attack strategies. For example, a social worker who can't seem to get anywhere with her superiors may become hostile and cynical towards her clients, criticizing everything and everyone. More subtle are forms of self-attack in which we deal with stress by putting ourselves down and becoming unnecessarily self-critical.

Attack and avoidance are two basic ways of defending against stress. In fact, they are so fundamental that stress itself was once defined as the "fight" (attack) or "flight" (avoidance) response (Cannon, 1932) . However, attack and avoidance is are usually not effectively targeted to the source of the problem, and they are strategies we first learn in childhood. Put differently, they are generic all-purpose strategies we are most likely to use unthinkingly and out of habit.

COPING, ASSERTIVENESS, AND PEOPLE STRESS

The difference between defense and coping can be particularly apparent when dealing with stress involving others. Here coping involves effectively expressing and acting on your thoughts and feelings. Attack becomes aggression and avoidance non-assertiveness. These three ways of dealing with people stress--assertiveness, non-assertiveness, and aggression--are summarized below.

Two assertive goals are the key to coping: (1) to maturely seek to change a stress situation, and (2) to make known wants, thoughts, and feelings. We can call these *problem-solving* and *self-expression* goals. Often it is not possible to achieve both goals. For example, an acquaintance may have borrowed some money. Asking for the money back meets the goal of self-expression, even though the problem-solving goal of retrieving the loan may not be met. Both goals must be pursued in a way that is appropriate and serves your best interests. Asking for a raise when the boss is in an angry mood is asking for failure. Giving negative feedback when a friend is already upset or sad can cause needless distress.

There are good goals and bad goals. An effective goal follows the Sergeant Friday SCRIPT rules we presented earlier. Here they are again.

SIMPLE

Rule. Does your goal focus on one or two things rather than an entire "laundry list" of wishes.

Good goal. "Please clean up the grass trimmings after you mow the lawn."

Needs work. "I want you to mow the lawn before it rains, pick up the clippings, clean your room, come home on time, stop taking me for granted, and pay more attention to your family."

CONCRETE

Rule. Does your goal focus on concrete, observable behaviors and events? Does it indicate who, when, what, and where? Do you avoid the use of psychoanalyzing, use of vague and abstract terms, emotional outbursts, name-calling, or overstating?

Good goal. "I would like to get together tonight to see if we can figure out how to spend more time together this weekend."

Needs work. "Gee, I would people would stop treating me as if I didn't exist."

REALISTIC

Rule. Is your goal realistic or unattainable and excessive? Have you included the facts of the situation, rather than guesses, innuendos, rumors, and so on?

Good goal. "I would appreciate it if you could refrain from mentioning my recent stomach operation at the next party."

Needs work. "Please give me the attention I deserve."

IMPORTANT

Rule. Have you identified what is truly important to you? Have you focused on the real problem, rather than just the symptom. Have you identified the cause, rather than a relatively unimportant effect?

Good goal. "You failed to tell me you were going away this weekend. I felt left alone."

Needs work. "I feel so alone. I wish I knew what medication I should be taking."

PERSONAL

Rule. Is it significant to you?

Good goal. "You borrowed my suit last week. I need the suit for an interview next week."

Needs work. "Please stop treating your boss like he doesn't know anything. I'm sure he doesn't enjoy being treated this way."

TIMELY

Rule. Is the problem recent, or is it history and "water under the bridge"?

Good goal. "Today you interrupted me before I could tell you my problem."

Needs work. "Remember my birthday two months ago. I was really concerned that you didn't think to call."

Non-assertive people do not express themselves. They do not stand up for themselves and give in to others. Their goals are to please, not to "make waves," to avoid trouble, and to "be a nice person." Aggressive people may well express their wants, thoughts, and feelings, but they do so at the expense of others. Their goals become to dominate, manipulate, control, and even hurt. By not considering the other person, they create needless conflict and tension.

There is another way of looking a these three types of behavior. The assertive role is that of an adult seeking to solve problems, negotiate, or communicate in a mature fashion. You are a peer, equal, and colleague. The non-assertive role is closer to that of a child. You see yourself as inferior and submissive, someone who is controlled, manipulated, or victimized. You treat the other person's goals as most important. The aggressive role is that of a domineering parent, a manipulator, or attacker. The other person's goals can be ignored.

Finally, if you examine your Behavior Lines, you may discover that much assertive behavior is nonverbal. Such nonverbals include direct eye contact, a frank and open facial expression, appropriate voice and speech, a comfortable upright posture, and gestures emphasizing key words. Non-assertive nonverbals include looking away or down, constant nervous smiling, quiet and mumbled speech, slumped posture, and restless fidgeting. The aggressive person is more likely to stare and look down, clench teeth, speak too loud, stand too close and make a fist, shake his or head, and so on. Here is a summary of assertive, non-assertive, and aggressive behavior (Alberti and Emmons, 1978; Bower and Bower, 1976; Jakubowski and Lange, 1978):

ASSERTIVENESS

Your goals. Problem-solving and self-expression; You seek to realistically and maturely change a stress situation and express your wants, thoughts, and feelings; you act in your own best interests.

Your role. An adult, peer, equal, colleague.

Nonverbals.

Eye contact: comfortably direct

Facial expression: frank, open

Voice and speech: firm, warm, clear, expressive, proper emphasis of key words

Posture: standing, sitting upright

Gestures: emphasizes key words

NON-ASSERTIVENESS

Your goals. You don't express your wants, thoughts, and feelings; You give into others and don't act in your own best interests; You seek to please, not to "make waves," to avoid trouble, to "be a nice person"

Your role. someone inferior, a child, submissive, someone controlled or manipulated

Nonverbals.

Eye contact: looking away or down, blinking

Facial expression: constant smiling; smiling or laughing when expressing negative feelings; swallowing or clearing throat

Voice and speech: quiet, mumbled, whiny, monotone, too slow, too fast

Posture: slumped, turned away, stiff, standing too far away

Gestures: fidgeting, covering mouth with hand; nodding head; pacing or shifting around; restless playing with tie, hair clip, etc.

AGGRESSIVENESS

Your goals. To dominate, control, manipulate, hurt; You may well express yourself or act on your wants, thoughts, and feelings, but you do so at the expense of others; You do not consider the other person, creating unnecessary resentment and conflict.

Your role. Someone superior, a parent, domineering, controlling

Nonverbals.

Eye contact: Staring, looking down, looking away impatiently

Facial expression: clenching teeth; pursed, tight lips; sneering smile

Voice and Speech: too loud, rapid, sarcastic, silent

Posture: standing too close or far away; leaning over or towards other person

Gestures: making fist; finger pointing; shaking head; hands on hips

Defensive behavior may not only fail to contribute to effective problem-solving or communication, but it can also actually contribute to stress. To illustrate, the non-assertive person risks being taken advantage of by others. Wants and feelings that are not expressed do not magically go away, but linger, often causing continued upset. Non-assertive people often lose the respect of others because they do not stand up for themselves. At the very least, they end up becoming "faceless people," lonely individuals who are not known simply because they do not make themselves heard.

In contrast, the aggressive person risks turning others off. Such individuals can feel guilty or upset over their outbursts, wishing they had behaved otherwise. Although aggressive people may think they are actively seeking to meet their needs, they often work against themselves. Others are less likely to help those who come across in a threatening manner, and aggressive emotionality can cloud or mask the point one is trying to make.

Defensive behavior is most likely to be a problem when it is a habit over which we have little control. In contrast, defensive behavior can be self-enhancing when it is a choice, that is, when you are capable of acting assertively, but decide that this option is not appropriate. For example, a person recovering from heart surgery who temporarily avoids dealing with the implications of surgery may indeed have a better recovery. In addition, defensive denial can serve as temporary self-protection, a way of pacing yourself so you are exposed to only as much stress as you can handle at one time. Finally, there are times when doing nothing is a harmless option. Some stress situations simply can't be changed (serious illness, loss of a friend, etc.). Doing nothing is not only harmless, but might even help you from becoming overwhelmed and give you time to pull together whatever resources you have. In sum, assertive behavior is designed to be *effective*. To be effective, you must know the appropriate time and place to act, and when inaction is called for.

Few people are assertive in all situations. Indeed there are a large number of studies that have used sophisticated statistics to identify different types of assertiveness situations. I have summarized their findings into the following 12 types of interpersonal stress situations, ranked according to difficulty. They fall into three groups: direct communication and interaction, requests and negotiation, and conflict. For each, I have supplied three examples illustrating assertive, aggressive and non-assertive behavior (Bower and Bower, 1976; Jakubowski and Lange, 1978). Can you identify which is which?

DIRECT COMMUNICATION AND INTERACTION

Meeting and Getting to Know Someone

Example 1. You are at a cocktail party and see a stranger you would like to meet. This person is alone at the refreshments table. You decide the best tactic would be to stand apart from your friends, so he won't get the impression you're already on a date, politely look in his direction, and smile if he looks back.

Example 2. You have just been introduced to a new coworker, someone you would like to get to know better. Both of you have sat down in the cafeteria for coffee. After a pause, you decide to break the ice and ask, "Well, you're sure the silent type. Cat got your tongue?"

Example 3. You are sitting next to a stranger on the plane. After 30 minutes of small talk, you decide you would like to meet. You say, "We've talked for about half an hour and haven't introduced ourselves. My name is John."

Comments. Example 1 illustrates a common tactic non-assertive people use in getting to know others--hinting. Sometimes it works, sometimes it doesn't. It often wastes an awful lot of time. What's wrong with simply walking up to the person and introducing yourself? Example 2 is a bit more direct; at least they are talking. However, the ice-breaking question ("Cat got your tongue?") is actually a bit aggressive. It also illustrates the "closed question" in which the other person is given little chance of continuing the conversation with more than a simple "yes" or "no." Example 3 is simple and assertive.

Expressing Positive Feelings

Example 4. A friend has recently gone through a divorce and is feeling bad. You are concerned about her feelings, and do not like seeing her upset. Although you feel a bit awkward expressing your feelings, you have decided, "I have thought this through, and really care for my friend. I've been through a divorce myself and understand what she might be feeling. I would really like to help. If she asks for my company, I will me more than happy to spend some time with her."

Example 5. Your secretary has been putting in extra hours so that this year's deadlines will be met. You appreciate the work and initiative she has taken. You say, "I want you to know how grateful I am that you have been working evenings this week. You are doing an excellent job."

Example 6. You are on your third date with someone you really like. You have had a number of good conversations and really enjoy this person's company. You would like to go on another date. You turn to your friend and say, "I suppose you have something planned for next weekend. You always seem to hang around with so many other people."

Comments. Example 4 certainly illustrates kindness and generosity. But, unless it is actually stated, it simply is not assertive. In contrast, Example 5 demonstrates a forthright assertive compliment. Notice that it is not vague and general ("I think you are a super secretary. Keep it up."), but actually specifies the behavior being complimented. Finally, Example 6 almost borders on being aggressive. It could be perceived as an accusation or challenge to defend oneself. At the very least, it is a manipulation, a way of getting the other person to pop the question (i.e., by answering, "No, I don't have a date. Let's go out."). It would be much more assertive to simply get to the point and make a date.

Expressing Sadness, Fear, or Anxiety

Example 7. You are a supervisor at a factory and have decided you have to lay off one of your employees. This will not be easy, given this person has worked for your business for years. You confide in your roommate (who does not work with you): "You know, I feel really sad laying him off. But there is no other choice. He has failed to show up at least once a week for several months. His sales figures have fallen considerably. And I've given him three warnings carefully explaining his problem behaviors and the consequences of not changing. This makes me feel really bad."

Example 8. You are going on a new job interview. It is for a position for which you are only partially prepared. You've never done this before and are worried about being asked questions you cannot answer. When asked by a friend about the interview, you chuckle nervously and say "I really want you to know this--I appreciate your concern. I *guess* things will come out OK. I'll survive. You know me, I can deal with these things."

Example 9. You have been scheduled for a minor operation. Since this is your first operation, you are a bit afraid. Your girlfriend asks you if you are concerned about the surgery. You reply, "Let me be frank. I'm no weakling! I'm going to be just fine."

Comments. Example 7 illustrates a frank, honest sharing of feelings of sadness. This assertive encounter lets us know the feelings and the reasons behind them. Example 8 appears to start assertively ("I really want you to know this."), but the becomes politely non-assertive. But politeness is not necessarily the same as assertiveness. The negative feelings are only hinted at ("I guess things will come out OK."). Example 9 illustrates what can only be called dishonest aggression.

Expressing Opinions

Example 10. You are at a business meeting discussing marketing strategies. You are somewhat new to the organization, and everyone else has more experience than you. The boss is explaining her ideas on how to improve sales, and then opens the discussion for ideas from everyone else. You think you see a problem with one of the ideas presented, but decide not to speak out. You think, "disagreeing with the boss at this time might be seen as disrespect. I definitely want it known that I am a good team player and not a 'rebel.'"

Example 11. Your 16-year old daughter is shopping for a hat. She is eyeing an inexpensive, but somewhat showy piece covered with artificial flowers. You comment, "You're not going to buy *that*, are you?"

Example 12. You are attending a lecture by an expert in your area of work. She has made one claim you simply cannot accept. After the talk, she opens the lecture to discussion. In front of over 75 peers, you raise your hand and say, "I'm not sure I agree with one of your points. According to my notes, you believe . . . ."

Comments. It is important not to confuse respect and deference. We all, of course, have the right to be respected. However, in Example 10, non-assertive deference appears to be the result of feelings of intimidation. It should be noted that this situation is a bit tricky; can you think of circumstances in which it might be OK to be non-assertive or aggressive? In contrast, Example 11 is a bit aggressive. A desire is hinted at ("You're not going to buy that, are you?"), and presented in a way that puts the daughter down. Finally, Example 12 illustrates a direct and assertive inquiry. It is appropriate, since the speaker has opened the lecture for discussion. The speaker may well feel challenged, and perhaps even threatened, by what might be said. However, in this context, you are not responsible for their feelings. After all, the speaker has opened the lecture to discussion.

REQUESTS AND NEGOTIATION

Making Requests

Example 13. You and your date are trying to figure out how to spend the evening. He suggests a movie or going to a local tavern. You comment, "Boy, am I hungry." He says, "You know, I really want to go to the movie down the street. Let's go." You say, "I have no problem with that," figuring that perhaps both of you could eat after the play.

Example 14. You are driving through a strange city and are lost. Although your car does not need gas, you stop at a filling station and ask, "Excuse me, could you give me some directions?"

Example 15. You are reading a paper with a friend. He appears to be finished with the sports section. Wanting to check something out on the front page, you say "give me that."

Comments. Example 13 presents another instance of hinting. It would be more assertive for both parties to put all their ideas on the table. Specifically, you could say, "I would like to eat first. And seeing the movie sounds good." Example 14 is direct and assertive. Example 15 might seem assertive since an honest want is expressed. However, since it is not clear the friend is finished with the paper, it is actually slightly aggressive.

Saying No

Example 16. Your son wants to take the family car out for the weekend. You have let him borrow the car for a few hours, but feel uncomfortable letting him have it for a longer period of time. You simply do not feel he is ready. You respond by denying his request. He begins to complain. You say, "Listen, I am responsible for what happens to you. When you're an adult, you can buy your own car. Until then, when I say no, that's it. Understood?"

Example 17. Every year, your friends at church ask you to volunteer time for fund-raising activities. This year, you simply have lost interest in helping out. Although you do have the time, you simply don't want to help. When they call, you say, "Gee, I'm sorry but unfortunately I have other plans for the weekend you need me. I'll be happy to work for you next year. Let me call you when I'm ready to volunteer."

Example 18. You have joined a committee at work assigned to plan major building improvements. For the last three meetings you have acted as secretary. This weeks meeting is about ready to begin and the chair turns to you and says, "To speed things up, I assume you won't mind being secretary again." You reply, "Actually, I would feel more comfortable if we could rotate the job. I think its only fair if each of us has a turn."

Comments. Example 16 illustrates a good example of domineering aggression. It would be more assertive to frankly deny the request for the car and give reasons. In Example 17, you may well succeed in getting out of helping at fund-raising. However, the dishonest excuses clearly make it non-assertive. A more direct reply might be: " I do feel your work is important, and I know I have helped you before. But at this time I would rather not." Remember, you have the right to say "no" and not feel embarrassed about it. Example 18 is assertive. Differences are presented in an adult, mature manner.

Negotiating

Example 19. You and the friends have decided to take a weekend drive to some tourist spots in a neighboring state. Each of you has a different idea of what to visit. You suggest, "Let's first list all our preferences and then see how many of our wishes we can meet. If we have too many places to visit, we can take a vote."

Example 20. Your spouse wants to do one thing this weekend, and you another. She suggests, "It would be nice to get out, and visit the grandparents." You mumble "uh-huh" while watching TV.

Example 21. You and several coworkers are trying to decide upon which computer system to buy for work. Some want a system that can produce publishable graphics. Others want one that excels in mathematical computations. After others have made their points, you shake your head and raise your hand gesturing everyone to be quiet. "Here, I've got the answer. Since we work primarily with writing reports, we have to get an inexpensive word processor."

Comments. Example 19 illustrates a good, assertive negotiating strategy: first list all the options, and then vote. Example 20 illustrates blatant noncommunication, let alone non-negotiation. Perhaps mumbling "uh-huh" represents a wish that the problem will go away if ignored. Finally, in Example 21, a word processor may well be the correct choice. However, it is aggressive to ignore the other suggestions.

CONFLICT SITUATIONS

Standing up for Yourself in Impersonal Situations

Example 22. You are seated in a posh restaurant waiting to be served. A couple is seated after you and is served right away, by your waiter. Another couple comes in and is also served. Your waiter walks right by you on the way to serve yet another couple. You decide to make it absolutely clear to the waiter that you have not been served and are getting a bit irritated. You put down the menu and stare at him.

Example 23. You are in a theater trying to watch a movie. A couple behind you is noisily eating popcorn. You sigh loudly. They keep munching away. You clear your throat loudly, to no avail. Finally, you turn around and firmly state, "I am getting fed up with your rudeness and disregard for others. Could you eat more quietly?"

Example 24. You have been shopping and have been waiting in the checkout line for over 10 minutes. You are the last person in line. Suddenly, an older woman with a shopping cart loaded with merchandise moves in front of you, apparently not realizing you are in line. You say, "Pardon me, I was already in line. I would be happy to let you in front of me if you're in a hurry."

Comments. Surely, in Example 22, there is an assertive way of dealing with this problem. Perhaps simply walking up to the waiter and saying, "Excuse me, but we have been sitting for a while others who have come in after us have been served." Example 23 illustrates how passive hinting often gets us nowhere--and can eventually lead to an aggressive outburst. Example 24 is assertive, with a potentially non-assertive twist. The offer to let the older woman in front of you is assertive only if it is your sincere wish to take her needs into account.

Offering Negative Feedback

Example 25. Your daughter and another classmate have been getting into fights in the school lunchroom. You are irritated that the school has done nothing about the situation. You meet with the school counselor and say, "I have asked the school to do something about the fights. It concerns me very much that nothing has been done. I much insist that you speak to both children and find out what's going on."

Example 26. Your janitor has been doing a sloppy job cleaning the floors. Several times you have pointed out areas that still need cleaning, but he simply doesn't seem to get the point. His sloppiness is getting to you and you decide a stronger approach is called for. You say: "What's wrong with you? Can't you get anything right? These floors are your responsibility to keep clean, right? Well, do it."

Example 27. You are a supervisor at a local business. One of your workers spends a considerable too much time chatting with friends during work. Once or twice a week you have noticed that business calls have gone unanswered because of this socializing. You have decided to note this in the six-month performance report due two months from now. Your objective is to provide clear, helpful, and objective feedback. Here is how your begin your report: "Although in many respects we are pleased with your performance, we have noticed on several occasions inappropriate socializing on the job. For example, on June 3 you were socializing for about one hour and two phone calls did not get answered. . . ."

Comments. Example 25 is a good illustration of an assertive, adult discussion among equals. Example 26 is an example of aggressive anger. It is filled with global accusations ("What's wrong with you? Can't you get anything right?") and putdowns. It is possible to assertively express anger, for example, by saying, "These floors still haven't been cleaned. I asked you last week and the week before to mop them. I am getting very irritated at this job not being completed, and would like it done by the end of the week." Example 27 would be assertive except for one problem: bad timing. Remember, to be assertive one must express oneself effectively, that is, at an appropriate time and place. Surely, it would be more effective to give feedback right at the time of each socializing incident, rather than wait for the six-month report.

Expressing Anger

Example 28. You think one of your coworkers has been quitting work early, leaving you with extra jobs to do. Sometimes you even have to come in over the weekend. You get more and more angry. Eventually, things get to you and you say, "You're always causing problems for me. Why do you have to be such an inconsiderate person? I think you should shape up and do your job."

Example 29. Your roommate often leaves her things laying around the apartment. This creates quite a mess and you have to pick up. You have had several talks about this problem. One day, you bring your parents home, only to find the apartment in complete disarray. The next night she has planned to bring over a date for dinner. You plan to be away that evening, but before you leave you deliberately leave the kitchen in a very cluttered condition, hoping she will realize how it feels to come home to a messy place.

Example 30. A friend of yours has the bad habit of putting you down in front of others. Often he makes demeaning comments about how you dress or comb your hair. You have asked him to quit, but to no avail. Recently he embarrassed you in front of someone you were dating for the first time. You were furious. The next day, when both of you are alone, you say, "Frankly, I am really angry at you. I was dating Chris for the first time and you made fun of how I was dressed. I was really embarrassed and thought you had promised not to do that any more. I got so angry I even felt like slugging you. I'm really pissed off."

Comments. The demeaning orders and vague, overgeneralized accusations of Example 28 make it clearly and overtly aggressive. In contrast, Example 29 illustrates a special type of aggression called passive-aggression. Here, one non-assertively fails to state feelings clearly and directly and relies on an indirect aggressive hint that is designed to annoy, upset, and even hurt the other person. Example 30 illustrates that it is possible to express anger in an assertive way. The feelings, although unpleasant, are clear, direct, and honest. The other person is not demeaned or attacked as a person. The issue is the behavior, "making fun of how I was dressed."

Dealing with Negative Feedback

Example 31. You are in a manager leadership training program. Part of your course involves making practice job interviews with your instructor, who plays the role of a prospective job applicant. Your instructor criticizes your performance: "You asked all the right questions, but I think your manner could be improved." You reply, "I'm not sure what you mean by 'manner.' Could you give me some specific examples?"

Example 32. Your boss calls you into her office to give you feedback about your written reports. She asks that you try to turn your reports in on time, rather than one or two days late, which has been your recent habit. Feeling a bit irritated, you reply: "You give me more time, and stop treating me like slave labor, and I'll be able to give you a report on time."

Example 33. You are in a very difficult class and haven't participated for the first few weeks. The instructor is concerned and sits with you. She notes: "For the last few weeks I notice that your attitude seems not to be the best." You respond, "I'll try to do better."

Comments. Example 31 illustrates mature, adult listening to feedback. Specific issues are discussed, and clarification requested. In contrast, Example 32 illustrates an aggressive explosion of emotion. Rather than sticking to the specific facts (turning in reports on time), negative feedback is treated as if it were character assassination. Example 33 presents an example of non-assertive compliance with criticism. The ambiguous accusation ("Your attitude seems not to be the best.") deserves clarification, but is avoided.

Dealing with Hostile Criticism and Anger

Example 34. Your supervisor comes to work in a bad mood. She gives you a stern look and says, "Why don't you ever do things right? I don't know why I put up with you." You respond, "Do you have to be such a bitch? You come in late, spend all the time talking with your friends, take two-hour lunches, leave early, and constantly complain about your damn aunt--you have no right to get on my case."

Example 35. A coworker has been avoiding you. You think she is angry with you for some unknown reason. One day, you arrive ten minutes late. She comments, "Well, at it again, I see." You say, "Sorry, I'm late. It won't happen again."

Example 36. You have borrowed a neighbor's broom, but have unfortunately misplaced it. Your neighbor angrily confronts you: "I wish you had told me earlier. I need the broom now. What am I going to do?" You reply, "I understand your irritation. I will be happy to pay for the broom, or purchase a new one for you from the hardware store down the street."

Comments. Example 34 presents a rather clear instance of aggressiveness. Let's hope it doesn't turn into a fight. Note the aggressive (and unfair) tactic of "overkill"--that is, throwing out a confusing and overwhelming torrent of objections instead of describing one problem behavior. Example 35 is a bit different. The coworker's hostile innuendos ("Well, at it again, I see.") surely merit questioning. To let it go is clearly non-assertive. Example 36 assertively acknowledges, but does not dwell on, the anger. Instead, the specific behavioral issue is quickly addressed.

CLOSING WORDS

You may disagree with some of our descriptions of which examples are assertive, non-assertive, and aggressive. If so, your experience is not unusual and actually illustrates an important point. Often there are no hard and fast rules of assertiveness. For example, in some circumstances complaining about poor service can be aggressive (such as when your 90-year old grandmother is slow at serving Thanksgiving dinner) or non-assertive (when a store clerk has both treated you badly and cheated you out of money). As we noted earlier, the *appropriateness* of your behavior determines whether it is assertive, aggressive, or non-assertive.

Similarly, sometimes it is not desirable to be assertive. There is a place for defensive behavior. The goal of assertiveness training is not to create mechanical, assertive robots, but to provide choices. Once you have mastered assertive skills, you can choose to be assertive, aggressive, or non-assertive. But there is a problem. What if your wants, thoughts, and feelings are passive or destructive? For example, what if you unrealistically think that having a date with the woman next door is an absolute and dire necessity? What if you think that everyone on this planet deserves your aggression because they are out to get you? Clearly there is more to assertiveness, and stress management, than saying and acting on what you think and feel. It is to this point we turn in the following chapter.

4

The Stress Dictionary

Here are stress scripts for two people, John and George. Both are encountering the exact same situation, asking for a raise. Both seem to be equally assertive. However, John experiences stress, while George does not. The reason why can tell us much about the underlying causes of stress.

John's Script

GENERAL SITUATION: Sitting down with the boss to ask for a raise.

OTHER PERSON: BOSS

    BEHAVIOR LINE: Opens John's employment record file. Studies it thoughtfully for a minute. Slowly looks up at John. Frowns seriously.
    SPEECH LINE: "So, what is it you want?"

JOHN

    BEHAVIOR LINE: Pauses and takes a deep breath. Turns to boss.
    SPEECH LINE: "I would like to ask for a raise."
    FEELING LINE: Very high level of stress, including general feelings of anxiety as well as such physical symptoms as back tension and sweaty palms.
    THOUGHT LINE: "He's going to think I'm a fool. I can't go through with this. I should have kept my stupid mouth shut! This is going to be a disaster."

George's Script

OTHER PERSON: BOSS

> BEHAVIOR LINE: Opens George's employment record file. Studies it thoughtfully for a minute. Slowly looks up at George. Frowns seriously.
> SPEECH LINE: "So, what is it you want?"

GEORGE

> BEHAVIOR LINE: Pauses and takes a deep breath. Turns to boss.
> SPEECH LINE: "I would like to ask for a raise."
> FEELING LINE: Mild symptoms of stress including slight feelings of irritation.
> THOUGHT LINE: "I can only do my best. If I make a mistake, it won't be the end of the world. All I have to do is simply ask. The worst that can happen is that he will say 'no.'"

First, John is experiencing considerably more stress, as can be seen from his Feeling Line. His discomfort includes feelings of anxiety, back tension, and sweaty palms. The source of his stress can be found in his Thought Line, his silent dialogue. John worries about how serious the negative consequences might be, and so on. You may have noticed from your stress scripts how important Thought Lines can be. They can influence what you say, do, and feel.

THE STRESS DICTIONARY

Not all thoughts are equally likely to create stress. Two therapists, Aaron Beck (Beck, Rush, Hollon, and Shaw, 1979) and Albert Ellis (Ellis and Grieger, 1977), have spent decades attempting to identify those that are most troublesome. Taken together, the most frequently mentioned terms make a rather remarkable "unabridged" stress dictionary. Here it is:

All-or-None Thinking

All-or-none thinking involves unrealistically dividing your world into rigid black and white, either/or categories, not leaving room for alternatives or shades of gray.

Example: Susan is going on her first date with Burt. While waiting for him to show, a host of nervous thoughts run through her mind.

> STRESSFUL THOUGHT LINE: "He will like me or dislike me."
>
> IMPROVED THOUGHT LINE: "We may not be perfect for each other, but I'll bet we can find something in common."

Example: Matt is seeing a therapist in order to learn to cope more effectively. He has had a problem feeling depressed when things do not go his way. Recently at work he had to rewrite a report because of a number of small errors. He began to feel down.

> STRESSFUL THOUGHT LINE: "Therapy isn't working. My old depression problem is returning. I really thought I would be over my problems by now."
>
> IMPROVED THOUGHT LINE: "Therapy takes time. It's unrealistic to expect that all my difficulties would be completely solved. Sure, I still get depressed. But it isn't as bad as it used to be--and that's an improvement."

Awfulizing

One powerful way to create needless stress is to exaggerate the significance of negative events. Sure, life is filled with frustrations, irritations, and disappointments, and it is normal to recognize life's hassles as well as its uplifts. However, we awfulize when we turn a simple disappointment into a disaster, a frustration into a catastrophe, and a hassle into the end of the world.

Example: Judith works in a local clothing store. Christmas is approaching and she was hoping for a nice cash bonus. When the bonus did not appear, Judith was crushed.

> STRESSFUL THOUGHT LINE: "My Christmas is ruined. This is the worst thing that could have ever happened to me."
>
> IMPROVED THOUGHT LINE: "What a disappointment. I feel frustrated and irritated I didn't get the bonus. I guess I'll just have to make do."

Example: Tom's family is coming to visit for the first time in a year. He want's everything to be perfect. The lawn is mowed, bushes trimmed, and walks cleaned. Tom has even painted the roof and planted fresh flowers. The day before the visit he spills ink on a small throw rug at the entrance. He explodes and storms out of his house.

STRESSFUL THOUGHT LINE: "How could I be so stupid! Now, I've ruined everything!"

IMPROVED THOUGHT LINE: "Oh no, what a mess! Well, my parents will just have to understand that no one's perfect."

Blaming

Blaming involves arbitrarily and unthinkingly throwing the responsibility for life's misfortunes onto some external source, person, or circumstance. You inappropriately blame others, point fingers, look for a scapegoat, and so on. Often, blaming can contribute needlessly to feelings of hostility and irritation.

Example: Jim recently failed an exam in his history course. Although he was clearly not prepared to take the test, his Thought Line reveals a different perspective.

STRESSFUL THOUGHT LINE: "That lousy professor. Always asking the worst questions just to trick us."

IMPROVED THOUGHT LINE: "I'm not sure I understand why I failed this exam. Was it a bad exam? Did I study wrong? Maybe I should talk with the professor."

Example: Bea is a social worker in a local clinic. Recently the clinic has been underfunded, and work assignments have increased. Many staff members are experiencing severe frustration and burnout. Working with client problems just isn't as rewarding as it once was.

STRESSFUL THOUGHT LINE: "These stupid clients. They never change. I try my best and they come back every week with the same problems."

IMPROVED THOUGHT LINE: "It is understandable that I feel frustrated with the increased work load. Sure, I have the urge to take it out on my clients. But it isn't their fault. If we had more resources, everyone would be much better off."

Childhood Fantasy

Childhood is a special time in life when our needs are taken care of by others and we can expect to be loved and protected by nearly everyone around us. Unfortunately, the adult world is a bit more harsh. Love, success, and happy endings are not guaranteed. Adults who continue to live in a world of childhood dreams are setting themselves up for frustration and disappointment.

Example: Joyce just gave a presentation to a church group. Although most people applauded, a few simply looked bored. Two left before the presentation was over. She became very concerned and upset over this.

STRESSFUL THOUGHT LINE: "Everyone should appreciate the work I am doing."
IMPROVED THOUGHT LINE: "My work can't be appreciated by everyone. Some may like, and some dislike what I do-- that's life."

Example: Midge is a high school student. For years she wanted to be invited on the debating team. This year, she doubled her efforts. She studied extra hard, making sure her grades were up. When she wasn't invited, she started feeling very upset.

STRESSFUL THOUGHT LINE: "You can always get what you want, if you try hard enough. This just isn't fair."
IMPROVED THOUGHT LINE: "Unfortunately, sometimes you don't get what you want and work for."

Egocentrism

To be egocentric is to think of yourself as the center of the world (yours and everyone else's). It is to behave as if you have some special status, or rights and privileges above what others have.

Example: Grace works as secretary for a local accounting firm. This week she received a critical evaluation from her supervisor. In addition, she lost the original for a report she was working on. We can see how her thinking contributed to her upset.

STRESSFUL THOUGHT LINE: "Why does all of this have to happen to me? What did I do to deserve this?"

IMPROVED THOUGHT LINE: "Sometimes bad things just happen."

Example. Johanna is driving to work. The person in front of him is driving a bit slowly. Johanna gets very irritated and starts honking his horn.

STRESSFUL THOUGHT LINE: "I own the road. Move aside, I have important things to do."
IMPROVED THOUGHT LINE: "I hope he moves aside. If not, I'll just pass him at the first opportunity."

Fortune-Telling

Few people can tell the future, and no one has a perfect crystal ball. And yet we engage in fortune-telling whenever we act as if we know just how things will turn out.

Example: Geraldine promised her friend, Midge, that she would go out on a blind date with James.

STRESSFUL THOUGHT LINE: "This date is going to be a disaster, I just know it."
IMPROVED THOUGHT LINE: "This date may not turn out the way I want. I might as well see what happens."

Example: Cecil lost a good job as an auto mechanic at a local shop. Business was down and the shop simply couldn't afford to keep him on.

STRESSFUL THOUGHT LINE: "I'm never going to be able to find another job."
IMPROVED THOUGHT LINE: "Although the future may seem bleak at this moment, realistically I will probably find some kind of work."

Helpless Thinking

One of the basic assumptions of this book is that there is always something you can do about a stressful situation. Even in the most serious situations it is possible to exert some control, whether it be through coping or defense. Such control might involve saying what you think, seeking satisfaction elsewhere, changing your thinking, or even acquiring a degree of understanding over or an ability to predict stressful events. Complete giving up, or assuming total helplessness, ignores the resources most of us have. Such helpless thinking aggravates stress.

Example: Jody has just said something has that hurt her roommate's feelings. The roommate has left the room in tears. Jody stands paralyzed with her mouth open.

STRESSFUL THOUGHT LINE: "I've really messed things up now. There's nothing I can do to fix things."
IMPROVED THOUGHT LINE: "Now, let's be reasonable. There's got to be something I can do to make things better."

Example: Ivan has failed his math exam. He sits and stares.

STRESSFUL THOUGHT LINE: "I just don't have what it takes. I have no idea how to prepare for the next exam."
IMPROVED THOUGHT LINE: "I really feel at a loss. I just don't know what to do. Well, let's see. Things can't be that bad. I'll either have to learn to accept a lower grade, or figure out where to get help. I wonder where I might go in school to get help . . . ."

Leaping to Conclusions

In general, leaping to conclusions involves making up your mind about something in the absence of relevant evidence or on the basis of incomplete, inappropriate, or purely emotional evidence. It is thinking in an oversimplified manner or ignoring important positive information.

Example: Mable has been a secretary for years. She is well-respected for her quality and careful work. One day, she turned in a letter with an unusual number of errors. When her mistakes were pointed out, she felt extremely bad.

STRESSFUL THOUGHT LINE: "I'm such a bad secretary."
IMPROVED THOUGHT LINE: "How odd. I've been doing fairly well. This mistake is really unusual for me."

Example: Beatrice worries about her 15-year old son, John. Although he is doing well in school, has avoided gangs and drugs, and wants to go on to college, he doesn't have a girlfriend.

STRESSFUL THOUGHT LINE: "I have failed as a mother. He isn't dating anyone. Maybe I should see a psychologist."

IMPROVED THOUGHT LINE: "I deserve to be proud of my son. He is certainly doing a lot better in just about every area than the other boys on the street. I admit that he isn't dating anyone at the present moment. But that's just a minor problem."

Mind-Reading

Many of us create needless stress by pretending we are mind readers. We often assume we know the motives, reasons, emotions of others, even in the absence of clear evidence. Such mind reading should be left to sorcerers.

Example: Bertha and her husband, Burt, are planning a weekend vacation. Burt has been rejecting every suggestion Bertha makes. Bertha eventually gets very angry.

STRESSFUL THOUGHT LINE: "Why is he trying to put me down?"

IMPROVED THOUGHT LINE: "This is irritating. I just can't figure out why he has rejected every suggestion."

Example: Fred is a new mechanic in a local filling station. His supervisor calls him into the office for a conference. The supervisor begins with this criticism: "Fred, I would like you to fill out your job forms in ink from now on. You've been using pencil, and some of your forms have become smeared.

STRESSFUL THOUGHT LINE: "He's just trying to embarrass me in front of everyone else."

IMPROVED THOUGHT LINE: "Oops, gotta use ink from now on. No big problem."

Minimizing

The minimizer tends to understate or discount the significance of a stress situation that is in fact important and merits attention. He or she may undervalue the importance of personal feelings, or the potential cost of an event to oneself and others.

Example: Jose has a problem with his neighbor, John. Specifically, John has the unfortunate habit of pointing out Jose's faults and shortcomings in front of other friends. However, Jose says nothing, not wanting to "rock the boat" and possibly harm relations with his neighbor.

> STRESSFUL THOUGHT LINE: "John just insulted me again. Oh well, it's not that important. I'll get over it."
>
> IMPROVED THOUGHT LINE: "John just insulted me again. True, this isn't a big crisis, but I'm irritated and have every right to bring this to his attention. It's OK to share negative feelings. I might feel a bit uncomfortable, but it won't be the end of the world."

Example: Maria is taking a class in psychology at a local college. She hesitates asking questions in class, even when she doesn't understand something.

> STRESSFUL THOUGHT LINE: "Oh well, my question isn't that important anyway. I'll get by."
>
> IMPROVED THOUGHT LINE: "I really don't understand what the professor is saying. I bet I'm not the only one. It will only take a minute to ask this question. Who knows, he may cover this material on the test."

Musturbating

Psychologist Alfred Ellis (Ellis and Harper, 1975) has somewhat mirthfully coined the phrase "musturbation" to refer to stress thoughts permeated with "shoulds, musts, oughts, have tos," and so on. We musturbate when we turn wishes and desires into absolute necessities. Few things are absolutely necessary for life, although there are many things that would be nice or desirable. Confusing the two creates needless stress, as is illustrated below.

Example: Tonya is a senior in high school. For some time she has been interested in meeting a classmate, Jake. Here's her stressful thought line.

> STRESSFUL THOUGHT LINE: "I'm simply going crazy over Jake. I simply *must* meet him. I would give any thing for a date."

IMPROVED THOUGHT LINE: "I really want to meet Jake. I would like very much to go on a date, although if he's not interested that would not be the end of the world."

Example: Carla is a nurse in a local hospital. Part of her job is writing patient reports at the end of the day. If the reports are not completed one day, she must spend a few minutes the following day completing them.

STRESSFUL THOUGHT LINE: "I have got to finish all of these reports before I leave today. I'll worry about them all night if I don't."

IMPROVED THOUGHT LINE: "I is certainly my desire to complete all of these reports today. But if I don't, no big problem. I'll just spend a few minutes tomorrow completing them."

Personalizing

Personalizing involves needlessly blaming oneself and viewing unrelated events as personal attacks. It is also arbitrarily assuming a personal involvement or responsibility for an unfortunate situation.

Example: Mary is eating alone at the work cafeteria. A group of coworkers is dining at the other end. From time to time they look in her general direction. The conversation becomes animated with lots of laughter.

STRESSFUL THOUGHT LINE: "Why are they laughing at me? What's wrong with me?"

IMPROVED THOUGHT LINE: "I wonder why they are laughing. I doubt it's me because I haven't done anything."

Example: Bill is part of a five-member work team assigned to write a report. One week after they turned the report in, it was returned with a request to "make major revisions." Even though Bill's role was neither greater or less than the other members, this Thought Line contributed to considerable stress:

STRESSFUL THOUGHT LINE: "I really messed up this time. I ruined it for everyone."

IMPROVED THOUGHT LINE: "I guess we all share the responsibility for this setback."

To summarize, here is the complete stress dictionary:

Stress Dictionary

All-or-none thinking	Helpless thinking
Awfulizing	Leaping to conclusions
Blaming	Mind-reading
Childhood fantasy	Minimizing
Egocentrism	Musturbating
Fortune-telling	Personalizing

Clearly, many of these forms of stress-enhancing thought are overlapping (we have presented all because people differ in which labels they prefer). One reason for the overlap is that all share two basic characteristics. Albert Ellis would say stressful thought is irrational. That is, it simply contradicts common sense, reason, or the facts. Therapists Aaron Beck and Donald Meichenbaum (1985) have said such thinking is self-defeating, that is, does not contribute to self-worth or health, or cannot be seen as a useful approach to problem-solving or defense.

OUR HIDDEN ASSUMPTIONS

How do we get to know the characters of a movie or story? How do they become familiar and real to us, just as everyday friends and adversaries? Let me offer this idea: each character holds certain enduring ideas or basic assumptions about him- or herself and the world. Such assumptions enable us to identify the villain, the hero, the workaholic career woman, the playboy, and so on. Often assumptions are hidden, revealed only by thoughts, emotions, and behaviors. Here are some examples:

GENERAL SITUATION: Julia often finds herself desperately in love, out of love, or seeking love.

BEHAVIOR LINES: Saturday, I went to local club alone. I introduced myself to every bachelor there. Sunday, I went to church. I sat by first single male I could see. I introduced myself to four singles during the coffee hour.

THOUGHT LINES: "I must have that guy . . . he would be perfect for me! My life isn't whole unless people like me. I've been rejected . . . Ralph didn't return my call. This seems like the

end of the world. I'll never find the right person. Gee, I hope people like me at this party."
FEELING LINES: "I'm lonely. I feel really left out. My heart is beating hard. I feel down and out."

Our stress dictionary shows that Julia engages in a number of forms of stress thinking, including awfulization, fortune-telling, musturbation, and so on. However, a simpler way of understanding Julia's stress thinking is to examine the enduring ideas or assumptions that seem to be guiding Julia's life. Here are some possibilities suggested by her Behavior, Thought, and Feeling Lines:

"People are hard to get to know."
"It is important to try to get everyone to like and accept me when going to parties."

In one sense, our assumptions summarize each of our own personal stress dictionaries. They do this by answering what might be called "The Why Question": "If what I'm thinking is true, why is it important and stressful to me?" Your basic assumptions enable you to say: "As a rule, this is the way things generally are . . . ." Sometimes the Why Question has to be asked several times in order to get to the real, underlying assumption (Burns, 1989). This can be seen in our example of Julia:

THOUGHT LINE: "I must have that guy . . . he would be perfect for me!"
THE WHY QUESTION: "Now, let's carefully think this through. If what I'm thinking is true, why is it important and stressful to me?"
THOUGHT LINE: "Because I must have a partner, someone who loves and accepts me."
THE WHY QUESTION: "If this were true, why is it important and stressful to me?"
THOUGHT LINE: "Because life isn't worth living unless people love and accept you."

Assumptions, like stressful thoughts, can become a source of stress when they are self-defeating or irrational. Psychologist Albert Ellis has devoted his life to helping people understand how distress is often linked to such thinking (Ellis and Harper, 1975). Here are several types of assumptions he feels are troublesome to many.

"It is absolutely awful if you do not receive the sincere love and approval of everyone."

"You must prove yourself competent or good at everything you do."

"Life is awful and catastrophic when things do not go the way you want."

"People who hurt you or behave inappropriately are bad or villainous and deserve severe punishment or condemnation."

Can you see how these assumptions actually combine several forms of stressful thinking? The assumption that "You must prove yourself competent or good at everything you do" represents all-or-none thinking, musturbation, and so on. The assumption that "Life is awful and catastrophic when things do not go the way you want" shows both awfulizing and childhood fantasy.

FIVE COPING QUESTIONS

If thinking plays such an important role in creating stress, how can we learn to think in ways that are more rational and productive? Unfortunately, society provides many answers that are less than satisfactory, for example:

"Just think positive and your problems will go away."

"Don't think about your problems. That only makes them worse."

"Relax. Things will get better on their own."

"Practice visualizing what you want."

Coping with stressful thoughts and assumptions is a little more complicated. Popular stress writer David Burns (1989) suggests asking a variety of questions, such as:

Question 1: What are your thoughts or assumptions? Which seems most important? How true is it?

When you are physically or emotionally upset, a non-assertive or aggressive, or encountering a stressful situation, ask yourself: "What's going through my mind? What are my stressful thoughts and assumptions? My Thought Lines?" It can help to write them down. Pick which seems most important and rate how true you think it is (you might use a 10-point scale in which 0 = not at all true and 10 = completely true). Here's an example:

"My friend Bill criticized me for showing up late for our date. I feel like a stupid fool. What's wrong with me? Hey, this is a stressful Thought Line. How true is it? Well, I'd give it a '7.' It seems pretty reasonable."

Question 2: What kind of stressful thoughts are you thinking?

Now, using your stress dictionary, try to identify the type of stressful thinking you are displaying. Let's continue with the above example:

"My friend Bill criticized me for showing up late for our date. I feel like a stupid fool. What's wrong with me? Hey, this is a stressful thought line. I think I'm awfulizing and personalizing--I'm taking this too seriously and blaming myself."

Question 3: How is your thinking irrational or self-defeating?

Now, take a closer look at the thoughts and assumptions you have written down. Carefully think them through. How would an objective, outside observer evaluate them? What makes your thinking irrational or self-defeating? For example, here's an assessment of our example:

"My friend Bill criticized me for showing up late for our date. I feel like a stupid fool. What's wrong with me? Let's be real and think this through. I have a good relationship with Bill. One thing that makes it good is that we are honest with our feelings. Sometimes he gets mad at me, and sometimes I get mad at him. Neither of us is perfect. Calling myself a fool just doesn't help things. It just makes me feel bad. I made a mistake and regret it. Life goes on."

Question 4: What are some rational and useful Counter Thought Lines? How true are they?

A central component of the stress scripting approach is developing short Counter Thought Lines for self-defeating or unreasonable thoughts and assumptions. Develop counter thoughts that are rational and useful. The goal is not to conjure up a set of "happy slogans" to repeat mindlessly. Our approach is not the power-of-positive-thinking system popularized by Normal Vincent Peale and W. Clement Stone. Instead, identify thoughts and beliefs that you actually believe. In addition, make sure your counter thoughts are relevant. Are they direct answers to your stressful thoughts? To return to our example, the following counter thought is somewhat irrelevant (although it may make you feel better):

"My friend Bill criticized me for showing up late for our date. I feel like a stupid fool. What's wrong with me? Oh well, I shouldn't feel so bad. I can be proud of myself for getting an A in school."

The following counter thought is to the point since it actually counters the stressful thought:

"My friend Bill criticized me for showing up late for our date. I feel like a stupid fool. What's wrong with me? Hey, so I made a mistake. That's not the end of the world. Nobody's perfect. And it was a small mistake anyway."

After you've come up with a counter thought, stand back and indicate how true you think it is, like this:

"That's not the end of the world. Nobody's perfect. It was a small mistake anyway. Let's see--do I really believe this? Of course I do. I'd give it a '9.'"

Question 5: Now, reconsider your original stressful thought or assumption. In light of your answers to questions 2-4, how true does it seem now?

Once we have a chance to think through our irrational and self-defeating thoughts and assumptions, our feelings about them can change. You can see this in our example:

"My friend Bill criticized me for showing up late for our date. At first I felt like a stupid fool. I really put myself down. How would I rate this thought now? Well, I can see it in better perspective. It gets a '3.'"

Here is another example of how this five-step procedure can be used. Take a careful look at it and see if you can figure out how each question is asked.

"Last week I thought I would call up my new neighbor Susan and get to know her better. She said she was busy and would call me back when she had time. I really felt bad. I'm such an unlikable person. Nobody wants to be with me. This is really upsetting to me. I would give this thought a truth score of about an '8.' Now, let's think it through. Am I doing any stressful thinking? Well, I seem to be leaping to conclusions when I think 'I'm such an unlikable person. Nobody wants to be with me.' Being realistic, some people find me very likable. Of course, I'm not good friends with everyone; no one's that friendly. And maybe she didn't want to talk because she has her own problems. My counter thought? It's pretty simple—'Now, don't leap to conclusions. So what if she doesn't want to talk? It's not the end of the world. I have friends.' This is pretty reasonable, I'd give it a '9.' As for my original stress thought? Hmm, I was saying to myself that I'm an unlikable person and nobody wants to be with me. Frankly, that just isn't true. I'd give it a '2.'"

We conclude with some more examples of Stressful Thought Lines and Counter Thought Lines.

STRESSFUL THOUGHT LINE: "I must be perfect and competent in all things."
COUNTER THOUGHT LINE: "I would like to do my best in things that matter to me. However, I won't base my self-worth on success."

STRESSFUL THOUGHT LINE: "It is very important that people accept and like me."
COUNTER THOUGHT LINE: "Let's face it, no one is loved by everyone. Some friends like me, and that's good enough."

STRESSFUL THOUGHT LINE: "If I work hard, I should be able to get anything I want."
COUNTER THOUGHT LINE: "If I work hard, I increase the chances I'll get what I want. But sometimes things don't work out the way we expect."

STRESSFUL THOUGHT LINE: "People who hurt me are evil and deserve punishment."
COUNTER THOUGHT LINE: "When I get hurt by someone else's actions, I should consider the chance the hurt was unintentional."

STRESSFUL THOUGHT LINE: "I feel so depressed. I just don't know what to do. My situation is completely helpless."
COUNTER THOUGHT LINE: "I feel depressed. Even though things seem dark and hopeless, my feelings may well be coloring how things appear."

5

Beginnings and Endings

In a movie, timing is everything. From the opening chords of
background music signaling adventures to come, to the closing
revelations of a long and detailed mystery, every incident is a link in a
drama's chain. The same is true with stress scripts. There are stages,
beginnings and endings, signals of action to come, and signals that all
is done.

BEGINNINGS

Examine carefully the following stress situation. Bill experiences
considerable speech anxiety when giving reports in front of class.
However, he has learned to deal with this problem from the very
beginning. First, he has discovered that his anxiety usually starts when
he opens his notebook to start working on a report. This is the best
time for him to deal with his problem, before it grows. Here is his
script:

BEHAVIOR LINE: I sit at my desk and open my notebook to begin
working on my report. I begin to open my notebook.
THOUGHT LINE: "Wait--I'm about to rush into this project
haphazardly. This is usually when the anxiety problem begins.
Now take a deep breath and relax. There are things I can do.
There's no need to awfulize. Plan one thing at a time. I have
enough time to finish the report."
BEHAVIOR LINE: I sit back, close my eyes, take a deep breath,

and relax. I start thinking of a title for my report and then plan an outline.

If we take a close look at Bill's Thought Line, we can see that there is something important happening. Early on Bill recognizes that "opening a notebook" is a cue for possible future anxiety. He then thinks things through in a rational and useful way. A *cue* is an event you determine beforehand as indicating that some form of coping or defense is called for. It is a signal for appropriate coping and defense, for putting into action rational and useful Behavior, Speech, and Thought Lines.

Using cues is a very natural thing, something we do everyday of our lives. Men often automatically adjust their ties (or hats) when passing by a mirror or window. Likewise, many women check their hair or makeup. Here, glass is an automatic signal for action. Similarly, in learning to manage stress, it is useful to select some reliable cue that warns you that it is time to do something about possible future stress. When you note such a cue, you know it's time to do something. Put simply, you note when to act.

A cue can be an outside crisis, your own physical symptoms or emotions, or even periods of worry. It can be what you, or another person, says or does. For example, if driving in a car makes you extremely anxious, you might decide that "sitting in a car seat" is a good cue for practicing a relaxation exercise. If talking to school children upsets you with anger, you might decide to use a pre-deter-mined coping strategy whenever you are within 10 feet of a child, or whenever you find the thoughts "children are awful today" going through your mind. The variety of potential cues is illustrated in the following examples:

The Salesman

GENERAL SITUATION: An encyclopedia salesman has called and simply refuses to leave you alone.

SALESMAN

BEHAVIOR LINE: Looks you straight in the eye and puts his arm around you.

SPEECH LINE: "I think you will change your mind about buying this set of books once you purchase the first volume. It's guaranteed. What do you say?"

CUE: The salesman's Speech Line, "What do you say?"

YOU

BEHAVIOR LINE: You reach up and politely remove his hand from your shoulder. You step back and walk toward the door.

SPEECH LINE: "I am sorry, but this has gone far enough. I simply do not want the encyclopedia. And that is final."

FEELING LINE: Frustration

THOUGHT LINE: "It simply doesn't make any sense for me to continue being polite, as if he were a guest in my home. It's OK for me to firmly ask him to leave."

The Airplane Trip

GENERAL SITUATION: Taking a trip by air makes you anxious.

YOU

BEHAVIOR LINE: You drive to the airport to make a reservation. You get out of your car and walk up to the reservation desk.

SPEECH LINE: (none)

FEELING LINE: Anxiety is beginning to grow. Your breathing becomes forced.

THOUGHT LINE: "Oh no, this is the end of the world. I know I'm going to panic and go home without buying the ticket."

CUE: Walking up to the reservation desk to make a plane reservation.

YOU

BEHAVIOR LINE: You calmly approach the ticket counter without hesitation. You focus your attention on breathing slowly.

SPEECH LINE: "I would like to purchase one ticket to Florida, please."

FEELING LINE: A little tinge of anxiety, but that's normal. I can tolerate it.

THOUGHT LINE: "Just one step at a time. Focus on your breathing. Just ask for the ticket. Just say the words, that's all."

Confronting the Waiter

GENERAL SITUATION: You have paid for your meal and think the waiter has charged you too much.

THE WAITER

>BEHAVIOR LINE: Abruptly hands you the bill and quickly turns away.
>SPEECH LINE: "Here you are. You may pay the cashier up front."

YOU

>BEHAVIOR LINE: You sit and stare at the bill.
>SPEECH LINE: (You say nothing)
>FEELING LINE: Fear of making a fool of yourself
>THOUGHT LINE: "I can't question this bill. I think it's wrong, but what if I'm wrong."
>CUE: The moment you recognize your fear of making a fool of yourself.

YOU

>BEHAVIOR LINE: You turn to the waiter, and tap him on the back.
>SPEECH LINE: "Excuse me, sir. I have a question about this bill."
>FEELING LINE: Some fear
>THOUGHT LINE: "Relax. Everyone makes mistakes. It is perfectly appropriate to question a bill. After all, it's your money."

THREE PHASES OF STRESS

In most general terms, the very chain of events that comprise a stress situation can serve as useful action cues and help us break a complex problem into manageable "chunks." As an example, let's begin with an account of stress familiar to many--the job interview:

Friday is Lola's interview. However, her case of the jitters began much before this, and lasted after. On Monday Lola's headaches started. She found herself thinking, "What if I blow this interview? I just couldn't live with myself. I just know I'll be asked questions I can't answer." This line of thinking continued up to the day of the interview. Then something new happened. She started feeling afraid and anxious. Thoughts like, "I've got to call in sick. I simply can't go through with this." started going through her mind.

Lola did go through with the interview. She answered most of the questions. However, she was asked a technical point about a previous job and was unable to answer. She froze, thinking, "I look like a fool. He now thinks I can't handle the job." The interview soon ended and Lola left. For the next three days she was depressed, thinking, "How could I have made so many stupid mistakes?"

What might be an appropriate cue for Lola? The question is difficult to answer simply because this incident contains several episodes. First, there was the waiting period before the interview, followed by the interview onset. In the midst of the interview, Lola experienced additional stress. And when the interview was over, the stress persisted. A stress situation is often like a movie plot; a single episode is not enough to describe what is happening. And different episodes may present different cues.

Psychologist Donald Meichenbaum (1985) has noted that a typical stress situation consists of phases. We will consider three: pre-stress, mid-stress, and post-stress. Each phase has its own cues, problems, and opportunities for appropriate coping or defense. The pre-stress phase refers to any period of time before the onset of stress. This can be months, weeks, or days. Here we are more likely to be preoccupied with feelings of anticipation concerning the future stress event. This is the time to emphasize planning and preparation. For example, imagine you have a major job interview next month. During the pre-stress phase in the preceding month you might find yourself thinking about the interview, wondering what you should wear, how you should prepare yourself, and so on.

When most people think of stress, they think of the mid-stress phase. Here the situation begins, and you find yourself in the midst of challenges. In a job interview, you are actually talking with your interviewer.

In the post-stress phase the stress situation is over. You may wonder how the termination of stress can possibly count as a separate stress situation? However, some important things can happen at the conclusion of a stressor. You can put yourself down for failure, creating more stress. You can fail to recognize and nurture budding successes. And, you may unproductively "replay" the stress situation in your mind.

Here are some examples of the three phases of stress. Note how the tasks of each are a bit different.

Going on a Date

PRE-STRESS: One week before the date, thinking and worrying how it will turn out.

MID-STRESS: The night of the date. You ring the doorbell, and proceed to take your date out to dinner. Later you go to a movie.

POST-STRESS: Your date has returned home. You are alone and begin thinking about what has happened.

Criticizing a Colleague at Work

PRE-STRESS: The day before you meet your colleague. You worry about what you have to say, and their possible reactions.

MID-STRESS: You sit face to face with your colleague. You present your criticisms and hear her reactions.

POST-STRESS: You have left the office and are now by yourself.

The Medical Exam

PRE-STRESS: You have a doctor's appointment next week. You think about what the doctor might find, and if the examination will be painful.

MID-STRESS: The doctor starts examining you. For about an hour she taps, probes, and looks at various ominous instruments. She says nothing. She then gives you her conclusions.

POST-STRESS: You leave for home. That evening and the next day you think about what she has said.

Every phase of stress can have its own cues, coping or defense goals, and Thought Lines. This can become clearer by examining the following chart (based on Meichenbaum, 1985).

PRE-STRESS:

Cues
The earliest recognition of a future stress problem.
Worry and anticipation about future stress.
Negative emotions such as anger, depression, and anxiety.
Physical stress symptoms.
Problem behaviors, reduced efficiency, and increased rigidity.
Increased defensive, aggressive, or non-assertive behavior.
A desire to avoid the situation.

Goals

To anticipate what can be anticipated.

To think through what I will have to think, do, and say.

To focus on the specific task at hand.

To combat self-defeating, irrational thinking.

To emphasize planning and preparation.

To relax when tension builds.

To "change that which can be changed, and forget about that which can't be changed."

Thought Lines

"Specifically, what do I have to do to cope?"

"I can develop a plan."

"I may feel upset, but I can handle it."

"Just say and do what I have to--there's no need to get too anxious or angry."

"Maybe this anxiety I feel will energize me to do better."

"Let's not take this too seriously."

"Take in a deep breath and relax."

"Easy does it."

"Just stick to the present issues and not get too personally involved."

"Let's not get preoccupied with worry. Worry won't help anything."

"It's OK to feel a little uptight."

"Just keep busy--it's better than getting all upset."

MID-STRESS:

Cues

Recognition that the stress situation is at hand and that now is the best time to do something about it.

Worry and anticipation about the situation.

Negative emotions such as anger, depression, and anxiety.

Physical stress symptoms.

Problem behaviors, reduced efficiency, and increased rigidity.

Increased defensive, aggressive, or non-assertive behavior.

Goals

To solve problems and deal with the stress situation.

To express what's on my mind.

To reassure myself that I can handle the situation.

To reinterpret stress as a constructive challenge, something I

could potentially grow from.
To remain focused on the task at hand.

Thought Lines
"Use this as an opportunity to 'psych myself up' for dealing with stress."
"Use reason to deal with my fear."
"One step at a time--I can deal with this."
"Let's not get too personally involved."
"Let's take a constructive, problem-solving attitude."
"There are a lot of coping strategies I could use."
"Just 'chunk' this problem into manageable steps."
"Relax and think of alternative courses of action. Then make my choice."
"There's no need to make more out of this than is necessary."
"Don't focus on my fear or anxiety, just what I have to do."
"This anxiety (or anger) is normal."
"Let's not exaggerate or catastrophize."
"Take care not to leap to conclusions."
"Try not to 'awfulize.'"
"Look for the positive; don't think negative."
"Relax. Use my relaxation exercises."

POST-STRESS:

Cues
Recognition that the stress situation is essentially over.
Worry and concern about what has happened.
Negative emotions such as anger, depression, and anxiety.
Physical stress symptoms.
Problem behaviors, reduced efficiency, and increased rigidity.
Increased defensive, aggressive, or non-assertive behavior.

Goals
To evaluate my problem-solving strategies and identify what worked and what didn't.
To find out what I can learn from this experience.
To recognize that even small successes are important. Don't put myself down for gradual progress.
To praise yourself for making an attempt to cope.
To keep trying; I can't expect complete success at once.
To avoid "putting myself down" for setbacks and failures.
To relax.

Thought Lines
"Good. I did OK."
"It wasn't as bad as it could be."
"I made more out of the situation than it was worth."
"I can see some improvement.
"So it didn't work perfectly. I can accept that."
"I can be pleased with my progress."
"Wait till I tell the others how I did."
"Next time I'll do even better."
"No need to exaggerate or take things personally."
"Even if I didn't get what I wanted, I tried."
"I did the right thing."[1]

The ideas we have been presented are an important part of stress management. However, you may be wondering, "What happens when stress is completely unexpected?" How useful are pre-planned cues when you suddenly get in a car accident, or lose your keys? Practice at anticipating cues can actually help you deal with the unexpected. You are less likely to procrastinate, wondering when is the best time to take action. You are more likely to recognize when you should do something, and when you can afford delaying action.

ENDINGS

The ending of a stress situation is just as important as its beginning. This is the time to reward yourself for your efforts and successes, and learn from your mistakes. Equally important, you can tell yourself that the situation is now over and it is time to stop trying to cope or defend yourself. You have thought enough about it, and it is time to go on. *Completion thoughts* serve this role. Such thoughts are not exactly the same as the post-stress phase we have just discussed. Post-stress has its own goals and tasks. You review actions you have taken, identify shortcomings and assess successes. Your completion statement truly comes at the end of stress. It is here you say, "Good. It's all over. I can go on." Here are some additional completion thoughts.

---

[1] From D. Meichenbaum, *Stress inoculation training* (New York: Pergamon Press, 1985), 72-73. Adapted by permission.

"I've done my best. I can't let this stress situation consume my
entire life. It's time to put it aside."

"I've coped and rewarded myself. There is really nothing more for
me to do. Time to go out and have a good time."

"I've followed my stress plan completely and now its over. It's
pointless to obsess about it any more. Things are over, and that's
that."

We are finished with our consideration of beginnings and endings.
Consistent with the ideas presented in this chapter, you might well give
yourself a small pat on the back. Good job.

6

The Stress Contract

We have finished our introduction to stress scripting and have considered six basic ideas: the Stress TEST, writing a script, assertiveness, rational and useful thoughts and assumptions, cues, and completion thoughts. In this final chapter of Part 1 you will have an opportunity to consider putting into practice what you have learned.

Perhaps the most important phase in stress management, indeed, the most important cue, is a commitment to change. One useful way of making such a commitment is through a written contract. A contact is a promise to yourself to complete certain actions, after which you will give yourself specific rewards. You might wonder, why not begin the book with a contract. Because you would not know what you are getting yourself into and the potential costs and payoffs of your decision. The choice to change can be an important one and should be made carefully.

First, let us consider some of the impediments you might face. We have seen that many thoughts can contribute to stress. These same types of thoughts can also contribute to resistance to stress management. One general type of resistant thinking is "nay-saying," or thinking permeated with "shouldn'ts" and "can'ts." The nay-sayer assumes that he or she simply cannot accomplish a stress management goal. Another general type of resistant thinking is rationalizing. The rationalizer gives him- or herself reasonable sounding excuses for not coping. Any of the forms of stressful thinking we have considered earlier can also contribute to nay-saying or rationalizing. Indeed, it is possible to rename our stress dictionary as the "Resistance Dictionary." We present it on the following page.

The Resistance Dictionary

All-or-none thinking	Helpless thinking
Awfulizing	Leaping to conclusions
Blaming	Mind-reading
Childhood fantasy	Minimizing
Egocentrism	Musturbating
Fortune-telling	Personalizing

Here are some examples of resistant thinking:

"I'm afraid I will hurt the other person's feelings." (Leaping to conclusions).

"My feelings are unimportant. I don't have the right to be open with them." (Minimizing)

"Other people might think I'm too aggressive." (Leaping to conclusions).

"I'm afraid to try coping because I might not be completely successful" (All-or-none thinking).

"I'm just no good. I can't do anything to make this situation better" (Awfulizing, Helpless thinking).

"I can't improve this situation; it's all my secretary's fault." (Blaming).

"Why can't everything have a happy ending? I'm afraid I'll be disappointed." (Childhood fantasy; All-or-none thinking).

See if you can rate these forms of resistant thinking:

"Coping will take too much time."

"One should always try to be nice to others, and keep one's feelings to oneself."

"More people will like me if I am not assertive."

"If I try to be assertive, I won't know what to say."

"It won't make any difference anyway."

"They will attack me."

"I won't be able to say what I want."

"Stress will go away on its own."

"My problems aren't as bad as they seem."

"Someone will eventually help me out and rescue me."

"I know all of this anyway."

Once you've thought through, and decided if you agree or disagree with your resistant Thought Lines, you are ready to consider whether to go ahead with stress scripting. This involves carefully weighing the costs and benefits to you and making an honest, informed choice. Non-assertive and aggressive behavior are not without their rewards. And assertive behavior can have its costs, as we can see below:

Benefits of nonassertion.
"People will like me since I don't cause trouble."
"I don't have to face uncomfortable issues."
"Maybe others will solve my problems for me."

Benefits of aggressiveness.
"I get what I want."
"People will think I'm tough."
"Others won't stand in my way or cause trouble for me."

Benefits of assertiveness.
"My thoughts and wants are made clear."
"I can get my feelings off my chest."
"People will respect me for being straightforward."

Now, let's consider the costs:

Costs of nonassertion.
"People don't find out who I really am."
"My needs don't get met."
"Others might think I'm shy and helpless."

Costs of aggressiveness.
"It turns people off."
"People might reject my wishes."
"It creates needless tension, in myself and others."

Costs of assertiveness.
"I might have to change my behavior and take risks."
"I might not get what I want."
"Others might think I'm aggressive if I go too far."

The same questions can be asked concerning our thinking:

Benefits of irrational and self-defeating thinking.
"I can delude myself into thinking everything's OK."
"I can feel important because of all the catastrophes I am in."
"I get attention."

Costs of irrational and self-defeating thinking.
"Problems are less likely to be solved."
"I create needless tension."
"Unsolved problems can create other problems."

Benefits of rational and useful thinking.
"More likely to solve problems."
"Makes me feel more in control; gives me a sense of 'I can do.'"
"I can enjoy myself more."

Costs of rational and useful thinking.
"Sometimes I have to plan ahead."
"It can take time to think things through."
"I'm not sure it will work."

In writing a contract, it is best to set small, manageable steps to be completed at specific times. Indeed, although it is quite possible to attempt a step that is too big, it is hard to conceive of a step that is too small. One series of steps might be to simply read each chapter in Part 2 of this book.

An important part of a contract is your reward for completing your targeted goal. One reward is simply knowing that you met your objective. But it can be useful to actually specify a tangible reinforcement you agree to treat yourself with if you finish. Pick something you ordinarily would not give yourself--a new item of clothing, a special dinner, a night out on the town. Pick a bigger reward for each level of achievement. For example, here are some rewards you might contract for completing the chapters in Part 2 of this book:

Goal	Time	Reward
Chapter 7	June 10	A pat on the back
Chapter 8	June 14	A special dinner
Chapter 9	June 16	A dinner and movie
Chapter 10	June 20	A weekend vacation to the lake
Chapter 11	June 22	A new radio
Chapter 12	June 25	A new CD player

It is important not to make this a chore. Make contracting a challenge, a way of having fun. Share your contract with a friend. Also, don't feel like you have to earn top score first time around. It's OK to aim for a lower score, and try again later. Indeed, its often better to strive for realistic smaller goals than for one big goal.

Part 2

Advanced Stress Scripting

7

Assertiveness Scripts

An assertiveness script enables you to think ahead in a careful and productive way. Nearly everyone has used this coping strategy from time to time. For example, as preparation for an important interview, you might try to anticipate what questions might be asked, and then plan your answers. And just before meeting someone new at a party, you might think through what your opening lines might be. Such preparations can help you deal with stress in a variety of ways. By thinking through what you want to say, you can be more confident in what you will say. In addition, you can minimize the possibility of forgetting important points. You can identify what might go wrong, and develop backup plans.

ASSERTIVE STATEMENTS

In developing assertiveness scripts, we will make again make use of *chunking*, or breaking a complex problem in to simpler parts. Earlier we used this strategy when we divided stress situations into Behavior, Thought, Feeling, and Speech Lines. Later we examined the phases of stress--pre-stress, mid-stress, and post-stress. We will now learn that an assertiveness script can be chunked into five types of assertive statements: Describe Statements, Express Statements, Request Statements, Interpret Statements, and Consequence Statements.

Describe Statements

In a Describe Statement you state the objective details of a stressful encounter, what was said and done. This can include the Speech and Behavior Lines of you and the other person. Here are some illustrations:

> "Yesterday when we were at the restaurant you said, 'I'm bored. I don't know what to do (other person's Speech Line).' Then you left the table to make a phone call without letting me know (other person's Behavior Line)."

> "I recall that last week you promised to return my book (Speech Line) but you kept it instead (Behavior Line)."

> "Last Tuesday I phoned you (your Behavior Line) and asked you to return the radio you borrowed (your Speech Line)."

Express Statements

In an Express Statement you share with another person your Thought and Feeling Lines:

> "I felt put down and a little angry (your Feeling Line). I began to wonder if you really cared about me (your Thought Line)."

> "I'm really confused (Feeling Line). I simply don't know what to think (Thought Line)."

Request Statements

In a Request Statement you ask for changes in the speech and behavior of others. There are three types of such statements: "I want statements," "I don't want statements," and "It doesn't matter" statements." These are illustrated below:

> "I want you to stop phoning me after midnight (other person's Behavior Line)."

> "I don't want you to quit phoning me altogether."

> "I don't really care when you phone me on weekends."

> "I would like you to return the book next week (other person's Behavior Line) and in the future please do not say you will return something on a certain date when you cannot (other person's Speech Line)."

In Request Statements, emphasize the other person's Behavior and Speech Lines, not their Thought and Feeling Lines. It is usually easier for others to change actions that can be observed by others than their inner thoughts and feelings.

Interpret Statements

Interpret Statements are like describe statements, however you describe the *hidden* behavior of others, your estimate of their Thought and Feeling Lines. An Interpret Statement can also address the requests the other person may be thinking and feeling about. It is important to note the difference between Interpret Statements and mind reading, one of the forms of irrational and self-defeating thinking described in Chapter 4. As you recall, both involve making inferences concerning the hidden thoughts and feelings of others. However, an Interpret Statement is clearly and tentatively presented as an inference, whereas mind-reading statements are presented as if they were based on demonstrated fact. This can be seen in the following examples:

Interpret Statements	Mind-Reading
"I may be wrong, but I have the feeling you are pissed off at me (other person's Feeling Line) and think my request is unfair (other person's Thought Line)."	"Why are you so pissed off? The fact that you think my request is unfair concerns me."
"As far as I can tell, you want to see a movie tonight (other person's Thought Line) but it doesn't matter to you if you go to a play instead (other person's Thought Line)."	"Ok, so you want to see a movie tonight. But, knowing you, it doesn't matter if you go to a play instead."

Consequence Statements

Unlike the types of statements we have just discussed, Consequence Statements deal with the future, with what might happen. Specifically, you describe the consequences to you and the other person if certain events occur. In script terms, you suggest what Behavior, Speech,

Feeling, and Thought Lines might take place. For example:

> "If you return what you borrow, I will feel better (your Feeling Line) about lending you things in the future. I can trust you to return what you say you will return (your Behavior Line)."

> "I will know that I do not have to worry (your Thought Line) and keep asking you again and again to return what you borrow (your Speech Line)."

> "Furthermore, if you return things when you say you will, you can feel better (other's Feeling Line) about asking me for help (other's Speech Line) and borrowing things from me in the future (other's Behavior Line)."

The statements we have considered are most effectively used in combination. We can now consider how to combine a variety of stress scripts. We begin with simple scripts and conclude with a more complex strategy, the DERC script.

SIMPLE SCRIPTS

The Impact Script

The simple lack of information can be a source of stress. The other person may not know the impact of his or her actions on you. For example, imagine you are waiting in line and someone has inadvertently placed their briefcase on your foot. The stress of this minor predicament may well continue until you simply say, "Excuse me, but your briefcase is on my foot." This is an impact script, one that describes the other person's Speech and Behavior Lines, and their impact on your Behavior, Speech, Feeling, and Thought Lines. The following example illustrates this:

> "At last night's party you spent over three hours talking and drinking with your boss and his lovely wife (other person's Behavior Line). When I asked you about your socializing, you turned to me and loudly explained: 'I'm going to do my own thing' (other person's Speech Line). This left me feeling alone (your Feeling Line) and wondering why I went to the party as your date (your Thought Line). That's why I walked away from the table with my dinner unfinished (your Behavior Line) and said 'I'm tired' (your Speech Line)."

The Empathic Script

In an empathic script you point out what you see to be the link between another person's Thought and Feeling Lines and their Speech and Behavior Lines. Put differently, you explain your interpretations of what is going on in someone's mind.

"I notice the tears in your eyes (other person's Behavior Line) and your comment that 'no one has called me since Jack left me.' (other person's Speech Line). From this, I sense you are feeling really sad (other person's Feeling Line) and may be wondering if other people are abandoning you (other person's Thought Line)."

"You have taken me out to dinner four times (other person's Behavior Line) and have even bought me a nice bouquet of flowers (other person's Behavior Line). I understand you like me and want very much to ask me out on a date (other person's Thought and Feeling Lines). However, I must be honest with you--I am already happily married."

Empathic scripts can have many effects in a stressful situation. Like impact scripts, they give you an opportunity to acquire potentially important information. In addition, they can help reduce the distance between people and increase the likelihood that issues will be discussed in a frank and open way.

The Clarification Script

A clarification script is something like an empathic script, except that you point out the links among *your* Behavior, Speech, Feeling, and Thought Lines. Clarification scripts can provide information to prevent misinterpretation and potential conflict.

"I didn't talk with you at the party last night (your Speech Line) because I was preoccupied with thinking about my big exam tomorrow (your Thought Line)."

"The reason I'm asking you to take my phone calls at work (your Speech Line) is that I will be meeting with the boss (your Behavior Line)."

"I know I must appear somewhat slow and tired today (your Behavior Line). I had to stay up all night with my sick daughter (your Behavior Line)."

The Contradiction Script

In a contradiction script you describe discrepancies and contradictions among another person's script lines.

"Last Friday you made a firm promise to have lunch with me today (other person's Speech Line). But when I called you today, you said you were busy with other things (other person's Speech Line)."

"For the last few months, you helped me clean the apartment every Saturday morning (other person's Behavior Line). This month you have been away every Saturday (other person's Behavior Line).

"Two days ago you promised you would not use the phone after midnight (other person's Speech Line). Last night you used it for an hour at one AM (other person's Behavior Line).

"Because you did not show for the company Winter, Spring, and Summer parties (other person's Behavior Line), I assumed you had no interest in them and didn't want to be invited (your Thought Line). And yet you say you are upset and angry that you did not receive an invitation to the Fall party (other person's Speech Line)."

Contradiction scripts can be the first step in problem-solving or negotiation, a topic we consider in the following chapter. They essentially provide the specifics of a potential problem, and give the other person an opportunity to clarify or correct problems quickly and simply.

The Mixed-Feeling Script

A mixed-feeling script is something like a contradiction script. Only here you share possible contradictions or conflicts among your script lines.

"I would really like to meet with you Tuesday night to see a movie (Thought and Feeling Line), but my mother is in town for only two days and I would also like to meet with her (Thought and Feeling Line)."

"I know I promised to let you borrow my car (Speech Line). However, it now looks like I might need it that evening (Behavior Line)."

THE *DERC* SCRIPT

Sharon and Gordon Bower, (1975) two well-known experts in assertiveness, have suggested a combination of assertiveness lines that are frequently noted in stress manuals. Slightly modified, their system involves four steps (the first letters spelling the memory cue DERC):

Describe

Describe the Behavior and Speech Lines of the other person that cause you problems. ("Last night you failed to return my car. You didn't call to let me know what was happening. You promised to be here at noon and failed to show up.") If possible, describe which of your problems another person could readily observe or verify. ("Since I had no car, I couldn't go to the grocery store. I had to pay considerable money for a taxi.")

Express/Interpret

Express your Thought and Feeling Lines. ("I felt irritated and let down.") If you are wondering about the other person's Feeling and Thought Lines, this is the place to offer your interpretation. ("I was beginning to wonder if you were somehow angry with me or were thinking about hurting me.")

Request

Next, request a change in the other person's Behavior and Speech Lines. ("The next time you borrow my car, please return it when you promise. If a problem arises, phone me so I know what's happening and can make plans.")

Consequences

Spell out what will happen to you and the other person if the requested changes are or are not made. ("If I can be sure of getting my car back on time, I'll feel better loaning it to you in the future.")

In following example, you can see how the DERC script can be used to deal with a stress situation.

DESCRIBE: "Last week you promised to take down messages for me when I am away. Three friends have called me and said they left messages, which I never got."

EXPRESS/INTERPRET: "I'm feeling very frustrated and a little irritated about not getting my messages. I worry about whether or not I can count on you. I even begin to question if you care about helping me out."

REQUEST: "If I can't count on you to take messages for me, please let me know."

CONSEQUENCES: "I could lose some very important messages if I count on you to take them down and you don't. I would like to know that you follow through on your promises."

At first it might seem like unnecessary work to spell out all the steps in the DERC script. However, doing so has some advantages. First, since you think through your script, you are less likely to miss an important point. In addition, your script's specificity and completeness is likely to increase its impact. By describing the Speech and Behavior Lines that are the source of a problem, you make it clearer to the other person what the issue is. Expressing your Thought and Feeling Lines adds a degree of credibility and seriousness to your script. By making your requests specific you do not leave the other person guessing what you really want.   And your consequences statement provides your perception of the incentives for resolving the problem.

Of course, it can be very useful to combine scripts. You may wish to combine a DERC script with an empathic, contradiction, or mixed-feeling script. The following DERC script has an additional empathic element:

DESCRIBE: "Yesterday, when we went on a walk, you didn't say a word to me."

EMPATHIC SCRIPT: "You looked at the ground most of the time. I was beginning to wonder, 'are you feeling OK? You seem down and out.'"

EXPRESS/INTERPRET: "I concerns me when you aren't feeling OK. And when we don't talk, I begin to feel confused about what's going on. 'Did I say something that hurt you? Did I ignore you?' Worries like these go through my mind."

REQUEST: "Please let me know what you're feeling, if you feel comfortable doing so."
CONSEQUENCES: "Maybe there's something I can do to help. I at least need to know if I'm part of the problem."

Here's a combined DERC and contradiction script:

DESCRIBE: "When you hired me as secretary, you described my job as involving typing and answering phones."
CONTRADICTION SCRIPT: "Since then, you have asked me to make errands, interview assistants, and drive to other offices."
EXPRESS/INTERPRET: "I feel overworked and a bit helpless. I'm beginning to wonder just what my job really is around here."
REQUEST: "I would like to sit down with you sometime this week and list just what my job responsibilities are and aren't."
CONSEQUENCES: "I think I can do my job better if I know what I'm really expected to do. And you won't have to constantly ask me to do new things, because you will know exactly what I can and cannot do."

Some scripts are better than others. An effective script follows the "Sergeant Friday SCRIPT Rules" we introduced earlier. We conclude with a summary of these rules:

The Sergeant Friday SCRIPT Rules

Simple. Does your script focus on one or two things rather than an entire "laundry list"?
Concrete. Does your script focus on concrete, observable behaviors and events? Does it indicate who, when, what, and where? Do you avoid the use of psychoanalyzing, or of vague and abstract terms, emotional outbursts, name-calling, or overstating?
Realistic. Is your script realistic or unattainable and excessive? Have you included the facts of the situation, rather than guesses, innuendos, rumors, and so on?
Important. Have you identified what is truly important to you? Have you focused on the real problem, rather than just the symptom. Have you identified the cause, rather than a relatively unimportant effect?
Personal. Is it significant to you?
Timely. Does your script focus on what is relatively recent and fresh, rather than history and "water under the bridge"?

8

Problem Solving and Negotiation

Hopeless predicaments can add to the drama of a movie or play. The heroine finds herself hanging precariously from a cliff. The mother of six loses her job, and then her husband runs away. The unfortunate babysitter seems to make the wrong choices when chased by the demented monster. In many instances your stress situations may seem equally hopeless, the stuff of soap operas and tragedies. In general terms, *Stress Scripting* attempts to give you control of a stress situation. All of the strategies we have considered have an overall goal, to turn stressful situations into problems to be solved or conflicts to be negotiated. We will now consider these objectives more directly.

PROBLEM SOLVING

The basis of effective problem solving and negotiation is one's attitude. Consider, for example, the following Thought Line reactions to a stress situation:

"Nothing is ever going to work."
"I just don't have what it takes."
"This is simply too much for me."
"No matter what I try, it will fail."
"I just can't think of what to do."
"There are too many things to figure out."
"All this uncertainty makes me too anxious."
"This is the end of the world."
"Because things are so bad, there's nothing that can be done."

Each of these thoughts reflects an attitude not conducive to finding solutions. Once one has decided to view a stress situation as a problem to be solved or negotiated, useful steps can more or less spontaneously emerge. A problem-solving or negotiating attitude can take many forms, including, as shown in the following Thought Lines:

"A stress situation is a challenge."

"Something can be gained from any problem, whether it be a solution, or the ability to accept setback."

"One day at a time, one problem at a time."

"For any stress situation, some solutions are more desirable than others. My job is to find the most desirable."

In this chapter we will learn how to utilize all of the ideas presented earlier for effective problem-solving. We will use a six-step problem-solving approach patterned after those suggested by D'Zurilla (1986):

1. Get the facts
2. Set goals
3. Generate alternatives
4. Choose a course of action
5. Take action
6. Evaluate the action taken

Get the Facts

What is the real problem? What information is relevant? What information is superfluous, based on emotion or interpretation, or not needed for problem solving? Once you have obtained the facts, identify what is problematic. That is, what is threatening or frustrating, how goals are incompatible, and so on. Here are some examples:

"Whenever I go to the doctor, I become very worried and frightened in the waiting room."

"When I experience a physical symptom, I start worrying about my health and wonder if I have some terrible illness. I need to decide what is a realistic concern and what is not."

"When my college instructor passes out an exam, I start thinking about all the things that could go wrong and become so anxious that I do not do my best."

"When my boss asks be do to extra work I would rather not do, I freeze up and just do it rather than object."

Set Goals

It is important to separate idealistic wishes from limited, realistic goals. It might be nice never to be troubled with pain again, to always get what you want when talking to your boss, or pass every exam with flying colors. However, for now try to set aside such wishful thinking and identify what you would settle for and what is realistically obtainable. In setting goals, use the simple facts rules described earlier, and identify main and subgoals. Here are some examples:

"I want to be able to wait for the doctor without undue anxiety."
"I want to be able to take an exam without feeling so much anxiety that I forget the answers to questions."
"I want to meet with my boss and ask for a raise."

Generate Alternatives

Now is the time to brainstorm. Put aside your critical thinking cap, and try to think of as many courses of action as possible. It doesn't matter if you come up with good or bad ideas. (In fact, it can be a good idea to think of a few silly ideas, just to get your creative juices flowing.) The idea is to generate many alternatives. How might others deal with your problem? How might a person you respect (a parent, teacher, or good friend) handle it? What is the most amusing solution you can think of? If you had unlimited resources or money, what might you do? How might a person with fewer resources than you successfully deal with this problem? Here's a brief example of brainstorming:

Problem. How to wait for the doctor without undue anxiety.
Brainstorming Alternative Solutions.

Practice my breathing relaxation exercise. Measure my stress level before and after to see how low I can get it.
Bring a good book to read.
Think about what I will do if my problem is more serious than I thought.
Count the number of leaves on the tree in the waiting room.
Bring a book of dirty jokes and read it while waiting.
Bring my portable radio and listen with earphones.
See if I can tell a joke that will make the receptionist laugh.
Try to take a nap in the office.
Write a letter to a friend.

Choose a Course of Action

Now put your critical thinking cap back on. Which of your alternatives are most reasonable? Rank them from most to least practical and desirable. When you have identified your top choices, think of what reasonable consequences you might expect and identify the pros and cons of each. Then make your final choice. Here are the ranked solutions for the brainstormed alternatives just considered:

Ranked Solutions.

1.   Practice my breathing relaxation exercise. Measure my stress level before and after to see how low I can get it.
     Pros. Gives me a chance to improve my technique by practicing it. Fewer anxious thoughts will run through my mind. I may be more refreshed after the visit.
     Cons. I've never tried this in a doctor's office, it might not work; I might fall asleep.

2:   Bring my portable radio and listen with earphones.
     Pros. I enjoy listening the local jazz station. I won't have to do anything to get my mind off being in the office. I can change stations and listen to what I choose, rather than the music piped into the office
     Cons. I might not find a station I like. My batteries might wear out. Others in the waiting room might hear the radio

3:   Bring a book of dirty jokes and read it while waiting.
     Pros. Doesn't require batteries. It will really grab my attention. Its hard to be tense and laugh at the same time.
     Cons. I might laugh out loud and embarrass myself. The receptionist might want to read the book too. I might find a joke that reminds me of my problems.

Selection: Bring my portable radio and listen with earphones.

Take Action

Now is the time to take action and try your solution out. Remember, this is an experiment, not some final test of your strength of coping ability. It's OK if you mistakes, or if things do not turn out as expected.

Evaluate the Action Taken

Most important, reward yourself for what went right. It may take some thinking, but try to identify what you succeeded in doing or remembering. Once you have properly praised yourself, identify specifically what you have learned and any mistakes you can avoid in the future. As usual, follow the Joe Friday SCRIPT rules.

Praise. I remembered to bring my radio. That's good. I kept listening to my favorite station even when I was anxious. I remembered a coping thought: "Just listen to the radio, let the doctor worry about your problems." When I started feeling less anxious, I said "good."

What I learned. Bring a radio and tape player in case I can't find a station I like. Do five minutes of relaxation before turning the radio on. Bring extra batteries.

ASSERTIVE NEGOTIATION

Negotiation can be seen as a form of assertive problem solving involving two or more people. It also provides an answer to the question of what to do when all involved in a dispute are assertive. Just as effective problem-solving starts with taking on a certain problem-solving attitude, effective negotiation stems from certain attitudes. For example, the following Thought Lines are not conducive to good negotiation:

"I'm right and the other person is wrong. There is nothing more to discuss."

"I'll try to get all I can, and deprive the other person as much as I can."

"This negotiation is a test of my strength and masculinity. My goal is to win."

"The other person is just out to cheat me, so I should not give an inch."

In other words, in order for negotiation to work, there must be a degree of mutual respect, a willingness to grant the other person the same "assertive rights" you have, and a willingness to compromise so that a solution acceptable to all is possible.

Goldstein and Keller (1987) have suggested that negotiation works best in an environment conducive to negotiation. Here are some of their ideas:

1. *Make sure both parties are reasonably calm.* It is difficult to negotiate when one or both parties are upset, angry, or anxious. It may be useful to postpone negotiations.
2. *Negotiate in a private setting.* When you are likely to be interrupted, or when others are present, both parties are more likely to engage in counter-productive behavior. For example, you may be more prone to attempt to save face, please others, and so on.
3. *Select a neutral setting.* If you negotiate at home, work, or some environment that is familiar and comfortable to you and not the other party, you have an unfair advantage. The other party is more likely to be defensive.
4. *Avoid time limits.* Artificially set time pressures can be counter productive and lead to lowering of goals, increased demands, bluffing, and poor communication.
5. *Negotiate face to face.* When you can actually see the other person, misunderstandings are less likely. You can see and read each other's body language, anticipate problems before they are voiced, and avoid the time pressures presented by negotiating over the phone.

Once the proper environment is established, negotiation is similar to problem solving. The following steps integrate the problem solving approach of D'Zurilla (1986) with the negotiating procedures of Goldstein and Rosenbaum (1982):

1. Get the facts;
2. Establish your goals;
3. Establish your position Request Line;
4. Listen to the other party's facts and position;
5. State and check your understanding of the other party's facts and position;
6. Propose, or invite, a compromise; and
7. Continue tentative "give and take" until you reach a satisfactory resolution.

Get the Facts

In interpersonal conflict there are usually two sides to every problem. It is your responsibility to clearly obtain all the facts as you see them. In time, you will need to share your facts, and attempt to see the facts as the other party sees them.

Establish Your Goals

When establishing your goals, it is important to set realistic, limited objectives. Consider what is fair to you and the other party. What goals are manageable? Are you willing to give something up in order to gain some of your goals? At this stage it can be useful to rank what you want and are willing to give up. Knowing your priorities beforehand can assist in the process of compromising. In thinking about your goals, remember that how you negotiate can have an impact on more than the problem you want solved. Your goals can influence your relationship with the other person, how much risk you have to take, and so on.

State Your Position Request Line

As we have seen, the third step in general problem solving is coming up with alternatives. This is also an important part of negotiation. However, it is a bit more complex. Begin by identifying your "opening statement." Your opening position can influence how successfully negotiations proceed as well as the degree of trust and cooperativeness between you and the other party. Generally attempt a moderate position in which your demands are neither too high or too low.

Listen to the Other Party's Facts and Position

Next, remain silent and listen to the other person's facts and position. Negotiation is problem solving among individuals acting as equals. Since neither party has more or less right to state their position, it is your role to listen openly. Goldstein and Keller (1987) have suggested a number of good listening rules:

1. Don't interrupt;
2. Don't "tune out" information you don't like;
3. Don't speak before thinking;
4. Avoid defensive distractions and deviations; and
5. Listen with the expectation that you will have to summarize the main point of what the other party is saying.

State and Check Your Understanding of the Other Party's Facts and Position

Often negotiations break down because of misunderstandings. So make sure you truly understand where the other party is coming from. You may first have to describe their facts and position. Let the other person correct any mistakes in your perception. You may have to repeat the process of stating your understanding and checking until there is agreement that at least both of you understand each other. Sometimes this is as far as negotiation can proceed. There are times when the most success you can expect is mutual understanding, and a willingness to "agree to disagree."

Propose, or Invite, a Compromise

When both of you feel you understand each other's position (it is useful to check this out by asking, "Do I fully understand where you are coming from?"), it may be time to consider a compromise. Remember, making concessions is central to negotiation. Both of you will have to give something up. But first restate what you want, being specific and factual. Explain your reasons. If a compromise is not reached, then offer concessions, beginning with those you have ranked low.

Continue Tentative Give and Take Until a Resolution is Reached

The heart of the negotiation process is a progression of tentative giving and taking until a final resolution is reached. This can involve a process of brainstorming similar to problem solving. Try to come up with many possible solutions. Once you state your goals and concessions, listen to the other person's goals and concessions. If a compromise is not reached, offer a bit more and examine what the other party can offer. In continuing this process, make it clear that your concessions are "tentative," and may change depending on what the other party can offer.

In summary, in true negotiation among peers, both parties: (a) understand where each other is coming from, (b) realize each other wants to maximize the achievement of goals and minimize making concessions, and (c) desire a resolution that is mutually satisfactory.

Problem solving and negotiation are somewhat ideal processes. What happens when such efforts fail? What do you do when your assertiveness script isn't working, or the other person has aggressive or avoidance goals. What are your options when in a no-win situation where no reasonable coping option is available. In Chapters 9 and 10 we will consider the problem of dealing with setbacks and relapse.

Relapse Prevention 1:
Short-term Failures
and Setbacks

Nobody's perfect. In dealing with stress, it is not unusual to encounter short-term failures and setbacks, times when your best stress scripts do not work or are not effectively applied. In fact, such relapses present important opportunities, cues to try again or learn from your mistakes.

Relapses can happen anytime. During the pre-stress phase you might find yourself "blanking out" and forgetting what to do. You may become demoralized with negative thinking. During the mid-stress phase unexpected reactions to your assertiveness may lead you to forget what you want to say. And even in the post-stress phase, instead of rewarding yourself for your successes and learning from your mistakes, you might relapse into self-destructive criticism. For each phase of a stress situation it can be useful to plan ahead a variety of backup plans for when things go wrong. Psychologist Donald Meichenbaum (1985) has emphasized that such preventive measures can often be the most important part of stress management. They can even serve to inoculate us against future stress. In this chapter we consider two types of stress relapse: self-sabotage, and sabotage from others.

SELF-SABOTAGE

Often when an assertiveness script goes wrong, it is because of our own thoughts and actions. Furthermore, such reactions can contribute to making a frustrating situation worse. We can deny our own rights to be assertive by engaging in "musturbation," rationalize away our need or ability to cope, or engage in all-or-none thinking and assume each small slip as a prelude to a coping failure. We shall term maladaptive and irrational reactions to setback as *self-sabotage*. Here are some examples:

"I can't go on."
"I am overwhelmed."
"I want immediate results, or at least the results I can predict."
"Nothing good can come out of this setback."
"Why aren't things going as planned? I must become preoccupied with this."
"If it's not a total success, its a total failure."
"If this doesn't work, then I've failed as a person."

Additional forms of self-sabotage include physical stress symptoms and self-defeating behavior and body language. You might find yourself perspiring, shaking, or experiencing an upset stomach. Your body language may communicate non-assertiveness or aggression, even while you are trying to make an assertive point.

It can be useful to consider the possibilities of relapse for all phases of stress (i.e., pre-stress, mid-stress, and post-stress). Generally, the goals for each are somewhat similar: to set up backup plans for when things go wrong; to prepare for the "worst case"; to stay focused on the present task; and to learn how to have at least some control, even when feeling out of control and overwhelmed. Below are examples of self-sabotage as well as rational and useful counter Thought Lines (many adapted from Meichenbaum, 1985; Goldstein and Keller, 1987; Turk, Meichenbaum, and Genest, 1983).

PRE-STRESS:

Self-Sabotage Thought Lines
"My stress situation is coming up too soon. I won't have time to plan for it."
"I won't be able to anticipate what will happen."
"What if my coping strategies don't work? I'll be lost."
"I shouldn't be tense. I should be totally calm, cool, and collected."
"What if the other person does or says something I haven't planned for?"
"I must know everything I'm supposed to do before the situation begins."
"What if I can't relax?"

Counter Thought Lines

"Even if I can't anticipate what might happen, practicing getting into a problem-solving frame of mind is a good idea."

"Now's the time to do my relaxation exercise. Now take a deep breath, and relax . . ."

"It's normal to get tense before a stress situation.

"Let's see if I can use this stress energy productively."

"I'll set aside just 30 minutes for worrying and planning ahead.

"All I can do is change that which can be changed, and forget about the rest."

"Just keep busy, its better than wasting time getting upset."

MID-STRESS:

Self-Sabotage Thought Lines

"Now that I'm in the thick of things, I have forgotten what I should do."

"This isn't working like I expected."

"I'm getting tense."

"There are just too many things to deal with."

"I think I'm panicking."

"Just as I thought, nothing's going to work."

"I know I've made a mistake. This isn't going well at all."

"This is a disaster."

"I just feel like giving up."

Counter Thought Lines

"OK, it isn't the end of the world if I make a mistake."

"I can use this as an opportunity to practice dealing with stress."

"Just remember to use reason to deal with my fear."

"One step at a time--I can deal with this."

"Let's not get too personally involved."

"Let's again take a constructive, problem-solving attitude."

"Just sit back and think of all your alternative courses of action. Then make your choice."

"There's no need to make more out of this than is necessary."

"Don't focus on your fear or anxiety, just what you have to do."

"This anxiety (or anger) is normal."

"Take care not to leap to conclusions."

"Try not to awfulize."

"Look for the positive; don't think negative."

"Relax. Use your relaxation exercises."

POST-STRESS:

Self-Sabotage Thought Lines
"This has been an absolute disaster."
"Nothing worked."
"I'm a complete failure."
"This was so bad that I'm going to just put it out of my mind and pretend it never happened."
"I really got tense and I was hoping I could handle this and be completely calm."
"I'm never going to learn how to cope better."
"Why can't I put this completely out of mind?"
"I feel like putting myself down."

Counter Thought Lines
"Even small successes are important."
"It doesn't make sense to put myself down for gradual progress."
"In learning new skills, its normal to have ups and downs."
"I may be upset, but I deserve a pat on the back for making an attempt to cope."
"Sure, it felt bad. But it wasn't as bad as it could be."
"This is not an absolute disaster; I'm making more out of the situation than its worth."
"So it didn't work perfectly. I can accept that."
"Next time I'll know what to expect, and can cope even better."
"It doesn't make any sense to waste time putting myself down when things are over."

In preparing ahead for self-sabotage, identify both your counter Thought Lines and Cues identifying when to act. Consider this script of a pre-stress situation:

SITUATION: Jeff received a low grade on an exam. He thinks the grade is unfair. For a week he obsessed over it, sometimes thinking, "Oh, it's only a grade. I shouldn't be so upset." At other times he really felt he was the victim and complained loudly to friends. Finally he decides to talk to his professor.
BEHAVIOR LINE: I walk up to my professor. We shake hands.
THOUGHT LINE: "I can't go through with this. The professor knows all the answers. Oh well, it's only a grade."
SPEECH LINE: "Sorry about my poor grade. I promise to do better next time."

In this script, Jeff's thought, "Oh well, it's only a grade" is a clear example of rationalization. It stopped him from planning how to deal with the grade. Here's a continuation of this script illustrating effective coping.

> CUE: [Here, a useful cue might be a recognized instance of rationalizing.] "I seem to be rationalizing. That's my cue to stop being self-defeating."
> COUNTER THOUGHT LINE: "No, it's more than a grade, its a matter of fairness. I have the right to know what I did wrong, so I can do better. And, besides, professors do make mistakes. I'll simply open my mouth and ask for a conference."
> SPEECH LINE: "Something's been bothering me. I would like to talk to you about it. Could we make an appointment?"

SABOTAGE FROM OTHERS

The defensiveness of others can trigger a relapse. Others can sabotage your assertive script, or even prevent you from thinking of one. Some defensive strategies are clearly aggressive, such as when another person blames or threatens you. Others are non-assertive, such as when the other person denies that there is an issue or attempts to distract you through changing the topic. Here is a catalog of strategies suggested by others (Bower and Bower, 1976; McMullin, 1986), loosely ranked from those that are non-assertive to those that are aggressive.

Non-assertive Strategies

The distracting tactic. The other person tries to divert you from getting your assertive point across by making incidental comments about you, what you are saying, or some other, irrelevant issue.

"You're getting so assertive!"
"What kind of perfume are you wearing?"
"You are so attractive when you are angry."

The "just keep talking" tactic. Here the other person simply continues talking, eventually exhausting you so you give up. Points are never completely finished, depriving you of an "entre point" for saying what you want.

"You may have a point, but let me finish my story about my vacation. We arrived home and had thousand of things to do."

". . . and the waiter was again late, and do you know what happened next? Well, he brought the wrong food and I just had to ask him this question. 'Are you too busy today?'"

"Then I went to the department store and took a look at these wonderful . . . (takes a breath) . . . dresses and decided I couldn't afford any of them but I did (takes a breath) decide go to the discount store next door where they had exactly the same dress and (takes a breath) . . ."

The denying tactic. The other person simply says your view of things is wrong.

"I never promised to take out the trash."
"What you are saying just isn't so."
"I'm afraid you are mistaken."

The minification tactic. The other person may hear your assertive point, but he or she attempts to control the discussion by discounting its importance or reinterpreting some important point.

"Come on, its just not that important."
"I was just trying to be helpful. Why get so upset?"
"What's the big hassle all about?"

The helplessness tactic. The other avoids your assertion by crying, playing hurt, or giving excuses by taking on the role of victim.

"I just didn't know it would upset you so much."
"I've been under so much stress lately that sometimes I just don't know what I'm doing."
"You really hurt me by bringing up the issue of our relationship."

The overagreeing tactic. The other person seemingly agrees with your point, often apologizing profusely for any wrongdoing he or she may have done. However, by overagreeing, you are prevented from completing your point.

"Oh, you're so right. I was just irresponsible for not showing up for our date. It won't happen again. I feel so bad about it."
"Yes, I know. You don't have to go into this matter any more. I'm wrong, and you're right. Fine."

"How can I apologize for treating you so poorly? I just can't tell you too much how sorry I am. Really, I am very sorry."

The silent treatment. After you finish part of your assertive script and wait for a reply, the other person simply does not respond. You have no reason for the silence and start guessing ("Is he angry, upset, thinking about what to say?"). Because you are uncertain how the other person is reacting, you find it difficult to continue.

Aggressive Strategies

The closed door tactic. The other person makes his or her point, and then refuses to discuss things further. The hidden message is an aggressive attack that says, "your point is not worth considering."

"I'm right, and that's that."
"It should be obvious to you that . . ."
"I want you to know that I'll deal with it in my own way, and that's how its going to be."

The joking tactic. The other person tries to "defuse" your assertion by turning it into a joke. By laughing at it, you are diverted from continuing.

"So you didn't appreciate my little comment at the party about your weight problem. I could tell--I thought you would blow up like a big balloon."
"Why was I late? Just wanted to see if your hair would turn any redder."
"So, you want me to dress a little neater. Why don't I just wear my tuxedo?"

The psychoanalyzing tactic. The other person plays amateur psychologist and avoids dealing with your assertion by trying to figure out your psychological motivations or reasons for making your assertion.

"You're so paranoid."
"When you grow up, you won't make comments like that any more."
"You don't want to see me Saturday because you feel uncomfortable with me."

The "debating" tactic. The other person tries to get you off track by becoming argumentative. He or she attempts to engage you in a pointless debate about some issue other than the point you are making or by reinterpreting your point in a way different from your intent.

> "You want me to turn my report in tomorrow? Why all this focus on my behavior? Shouldn't we be talking about what's wrong with this job?"
>
> "You want me to act more friendly toward your parents? Well, just what is 'friendly'? I am always friendly."
>
> "I think its unfair that you always ask me to change. How can ask someone to change what they've been doing every day of their life?"

The blaming tactic. After you have pointed out someone's objectionable behavior, they may try to rationalize their behavior by blaming it on you or on someone or something else.

> "Listen, I just can't be expected to be on time when it's so hot outside."
>
> "You want me to stop talking so loud to the children? Well, why don't you stop yelling at me? You're the one who always gets me worked up."
>
> "I'll tell you why I drive so fast when you're in the car with me. You always complain so much when we're late."

The verbal-abuse tactic. Here the attacker simply assaults you verbally by using inflammatory language. You are belittled, downgraded, and so on.

> "You're stupid to get so upset about such things."
>
> "Dammit, why don't you leave me alone?"
>
> "Your acting like a baby. You cry, complain, and do little else."

The threatening tactic. The threat is perhaps the most aggressive tactic to prevent an assertive discussion of issues. A threat can, of course, be physical. However, simple and often veiled, verbal attacks can be equally effective.

> "If you bring that issue up, I just won't talk to you any more."
>
> "I think you're asking for a fight."
>
> "I wouldn't bring that up if I were you. I think you might be very sorry."

Counter Scripts

What makes sabotaging tactics particularly difficult is the other person not only attempts to divert you from your original script, but introduces a new issue, one that may call for a new script. You are then faced with the double task of dealing with the sabotage, and continuing with your original script. A useful way of beginning is to briefly deal with the sabotage with a *counter script*, and then continue with your original script. The cue for your counter script is the recognition of the tactic being deployed. The following examples illustrate six types of counter scripts.

Persist.

SITUATION: A neighbor is also a door-to-door salesperson for a cosmetics company. While visiting you, she tries to sell you some brushes you do not need. You firmly but politely say, "This is the fifth time you have asked if I want a brush set, and each time I have said no. This is getting a little frustrating. I'm beginning to wonder why you are so persistent. Please understand that I simply do not want a brush. Then we can go on talking." Much to your surprise, she persists, "But I just know you will love these brushes so much. Just give them a try. They're not that expensive."

COUNTER SCRIPT

GOAL: To persist with your statement that you do not want a brush; to stop the sales pitch.
CUE: "My neighbor is using a 'denial tactic' by not listening to my request."
SPEECH LINE: "There, you have done it again. I am getting confused as to why you persist even when I make it clear I do not want a brush. But, just the same, I'm afraid you aren't getting anywhere with me. I must repeat that I simply do not want a brush."

Ignore what's irrelevant.

SITUATION: Last week you submitted an important work report to your supervisor without obtaining your coworker's input. Since you had promised to obtain this input, you clearly have made a mistake. However, your coworker is making mountains out of molehills and angrily accuses you, "I asked you to get my input first before turning the report in. You good-for-nothing. I don't know why I have to put up with this. This report had to have my approval and it didn't get it."

COUNTER SCRIPT

> GOAL: To focus on the factual content of the coworker's message, and ignore or dismiss the emotional outburst as irrelevant.
>
> CUE: Your coworker's verbal abuse.
>
> SPEECH LINE: "Let's stick to the facts. I made a simple mistake, and I feel a little bad about it. There's got to be a way we can fix the problem. Maybe I could send to the supervisor a memo explaining what happened. Do you have any ideas? I'm sure we can work this out so both of us will be satisfied."

Check it out.

SITUATION: Your secretary has been very busy on a variety of tasks. However, you've just received an urgent assignment from top management. A letter absolutely must be sent today to a new overseas customer. If the letter is late, an important contract may be lost. If this happens, everyone in the office may lose a potential bonus. You approach your secretary and say, "Excuse me. I know this is a very bad time, but I really need to have this letter typed today. Top management says it's important, and could even affect our bonuses." Your secretary replies, "What do you think I am, a typing machine? I'm sorry, I need a little more consideration than that."

COUNTER SCRIPT

> GOAL: To check if your secretary misunderstood your request. To repeat your request.
>
> CUE: Your secretary's joking putoff.
>
> SPEECH LINE: "Your joke makes me wonder if we've got a misunderstanding here. Did I come across in a condescending way? My intent was to deal with this emergency in a direct and practical way. After all, it is a problem that affects us all."

Note impact.

SITUATION: You are trying to explain to your partner why you feel you can't afford a long vacation this summer. He angrily replies, "OK, if you think we can't afford it, then we just won't do anything this summer."

COUNTER SCRIPT

> GOAL: To point out the impact your partner's angry outburst has on you, how it is not a particularly helpful way to deal with the problem; to continue working on vacation plans.
> CUE: Your partner's threat.
> SPEECH LINE: "When you say we can't do anything, I feel you are attacking me and aren't willing to deal with our financial problem. I don't see where we can get the money for a long vacation, but I would like to plan something. Let's see what we can work out."

Accept what's true.

SITUATION: Your mother want's you to continue living with her, as you have for the last 21 years. You feel you are old enough to live on your own. You say, "Mother, I have a job and can afford an apartment. Living here doesn't give me a chance to learn to solve my problems on my own." She interrupts, "But, you're just a child. So many things could go wrong. You just don't realize how important having me around can be."

COUNTER SCRIPT

> GOAL: To acknowledge what may be true in your Mother's comment, ignore the putdown, and return to your script.
> CUE: Your mother's psychoanalyzing statement.
> SPEECH LINE: "Sure, things may go wrong and you may be able to help me. But I want to try living independently, and learn from my own mistakes."

Present escalating consequences.

SITUATION: Your neighbor is a habitual "borrower." He has borrowed your typewriter, radio, and mixer. You have assertively asked for these items back, with no luck. Even your best

DERC scripts didn't work. You meet him and ask to have a talk. As you confront him about his negligence, he becomes quite apologetic. This has happened before and it gets you nowhere.

COUNTER SCRIPT

GOAL: To request for your items once again; to specify a set of "escalating consequences" if the items are not returned.

CUE: Your neighbor's apologizing tactic

SPEECH LINE: "I understand you are sorry for not returning my items. However, I have asked for them five times, and I need them. Frankly, if you do not return them tomorrow, I cannot lend you anything in the future. If it takes longer than a week, I am going to have serious thoughts about how trustworthy you are. If it takes any longer than that, I will have to ask our mutual friends if you have lent any of my things to them."

When Nothing Works

Imagine the tightrope walker at a circus. Although her performance might seem quite dangerous, she has a number a safety strategies. In case she slips, the balancing rod she carries can be used to latch onto the rope. She wears gloves that permit a stronger grip on the rope. If all these backups fail, there is a safety net to counter her fall. Similarly, in dealing with stress, think of a safety net strategy, what you can think and do if your backup coping strategies do not work.

One safety net strategy can be particularly useful when another person appears not to hear or understand your assertive point. As we have seen in all the examples just presented, the other person makes an attempt to prevent you from completing your assertive script. Often, the best solution is to process this maneuver, to change your assertive goal to questioning or challenging why the other person is not responding to your script. Notice in the example below how the original assertive goal changes to a process goal.

SITUATION: Marcie's mother been pressuring her to date the young man next door. Marcie has no interest in this person. When her mother persists with this suggestion, Marcie replied, "Mother, three times lasts week you tried to set me up with the man next door. I appreciate your concern for me, but I would like to make my own decisions about whom I date. I would feel a lot better knowing that you have some trust in my decisions." The very next day, her mother tries again to set Marcie up. It becomes clear that her original assertiveness goal, to state that she is capable of making her own decisions, needs to be changed with a process goal.

SAFETY NET SCRIPT

CUE: Complete failure of Marcie's assertion to be heard.

GOAL: To challenge her mother on her failure to listen to the assertive script.

SPEECH LINE: "Mother, four times you have tried to set me up with the man next door. I have carefully explained to you that I would rather make my own decisions, but you persist in trying to set me up. I would like to talk about what's going on here. I am confused and do not understand why you are not responding to my explanations of why I wish to be independent. I clearly state how I feel and what I want, and it seems like you are not listening. This is frustrating to me."

Another safety net strategy can be particularly useful when the other person's defensive behavior is so upsetting you that you cannot continue. Rather than abandon your script, announce that you are taking a break:

SITUATION: James has been dating Janice. However, his father objects. He feels his son should complete college before dating. In one discussion James carefully makes his point: "Father, I believe I am old and mature enough to start dating. Sure, I might make some mistakes. But how else can I learn?" Father ignores his son again, countering: "When I was your age my career and education were most important. I had the guts to put off dating until after school." James begins to feel more and more angry and feels like yelling at his father.

SAFETY NET SCRIPT

CUE: James' impulse to yell at his father.

GOAL: To temporarily end the discussion, making it clear that there is still a disagreement.

SPEECH LINE: "We have discussed this matter enough today. Your rigid perspective is just making me too upset. There are some points I would like to make. When we have lunch together tomorrow, I would like to continue our discussion.

A somewhat similar and considerably more drastic safety net strategy is to simply assert your point one final time, and close the discussion. This is illustrated below:

SITUATION: James has been a member of a local church for 15 years. He is also gay and has had a lover for 10 years. Church elders have been pressuring James to "go straight," and join their "homosexuality treatment group." James is perfectly happy with his sexual orientation, and has no intention of changing, giving up his lover, or leaving the church. He has explained this carefully to other members of the church. Each time they have responded, "James, we love you. It's your behavior we object to. The Bible is clear--you must change."

SAFETY NET SCRIPT

CUE: The failure of church elders to consider an alternative position; specifically, the third time they mechanically state their position while ignoring James's point of view.

GOAL: To make it absolutely clear that the disagreement has not been resolved; to make a final, summary point; to close discussion.

SPEECH LINE: "It is clear we are going nowhere. On three separate times you have asked that I join the treatment group. Each time I carefully explained that I am happy who I am, and have no plans of leaving the church. You and I have different interpretations of the Bible. As far as I'm concerned, we may never agree on this point. I choose not to discuss it any further."

Unfortunately, there are times when even safety net strategies do not work. We will consider this in the following chapter.

10

Relapse Prevention 2: Chronic, Unavoidable Stress

In the previous chapter we considered the question of dealing with short-term failures and setbacks. We looked at problems that are relatively immediate and short-term, for example, self-sabotaging thoughts as well as sabotage from others. We are now ready to go one step further--how to manage those situations which you know beforehand cannot be changed. These are life's chronic problems. Often they can be demoralizing and lead to giving up--the ultimate form of relapse. Anticipating and planning for such problems can contribute considerably to effective coping and defense.

To illustrate the management of chronic stress, consider these two examples. Imagine you have a backache problem. You have tried all forms of treatments and medications, all without success. Your pain is indeed chronic. Or imagine you are stuck in a frustrating job, one where assertiveness or quitting are not realistic options. Here your chronic problem may well be burnout. Chronic pain and burnout can teach us some important lessons about dealing with chronic stress in general.

Let's begin with pain. Most of us are familiar with acute pain, that which has a sudden onset and is tied to an outside stimulus or tissue damage. Burning your finger, stubbing your toe, sticking yourself with a needle are all examples. Chronic pain is longer-lasting, and often persists in spite of pain-killing efforts. Common examples include headaches, backaches, joint pain, and so on. Often the lack of understanding or control one has over chronic pain contributes to anxiety, irritability, or depression, forms of distress that can in turn further aggravate pain.

The severity of pain depends largely on how it is interpreted. Physician Howard Beecher (1959) was one of the first to recognize this. As a World War II Medical Corp physician, Beecher noticed that only about a quarter of seriously injured patients requested the pain killer morphine. In contrast, about 80 percent of civilian patients with similar wounds requested pain killers. Beecher concluded that the meaning associated with pain largely determines how it is experienced. For a soldier an injury has a somewhat positive meaning: he is alive and may be removed from a dangerous battle. Indeed, he may well be sent home. In contrast, the meaning for the civilian is more likely to be negative. Work may have to be interrupted, an unpleasant hospital visit may be required, and so on.

How we direct our attention can also influence the experience of pain. An athlete may experience substantial injury and simply continue playing oblivious to discomfort. In contrast, a retirement home resident, with nothing else to occupy his or her attention, may feel each minor pain more intensely. In other words, context can serve to direct our attention to pain, and intensify its experience, or divert us from pain, thereby lessening its intensity (Melzack, 1973).

How can meaning and diverting context play such an important part in determining whether or not we experience pain? One popular theory (Melzack and Wall, 1965) postulates a sort of pain-controlling neurological "gate" in the spine. The extent to which this gate is open or closed determines whether pain reaches the brain or not. A variety of factors can influence the opening or closing the gate: intensity of pain, number of pain stimuli, thoughts, and emotions. For example, you might be able to ignore the discomfort of a tightly fitting shoe until the discomfort reaches such a point that the gate opens. You then experience pain. If you are already in an irritable mood, it may take less discomfort to open the gate. However, if you are preoccupied with another pain, perhaps a burn, the gate may remain closed. In terms of gate control theory, meaning and distracting context can have a powerful impact on whether or not you experience pain.

Pain, particularly chronic pain, can provide us with several lessons on how to manage many forms of long-term and unavoidable stress and discomfort. These same strategies can apply to burnout. (Before continuing, it should be noted that if you have a pain-related problem, it may be worth your while to first seek the assistance of a physician as well as a qualified mental health professional. There are a wide range of approaches to managing chronic pain that go beyond the scope of this book).

STRATEGIES FOR MANAGING UNAVOIDABLE PROBLEMS

As we have done in previous chapters, we begin by identifying thoughts that contribute to the aversiveness of unavoidable problems. Some examples include:

"This pain is the end of the world."
"I simply can't stand this."
"There is nothing I can do to escape; therefore I am doomed to live in misery."
"Things just seem completely hopeless."
"Pain and discomfort are always unhealthy. This is not good for me. I'm going to suffer the consequences."

One of the first steps in dealing with unavoidable distress is to counter such thinking by taking a rational, problem-solving point of view. The situation may not be what you desire, but how can you make-do? How can you survive in spite of less than favorable circumstances? How can you go on living? We will consider three general strategies (Smith, in press): diverting attention from a situation, changing a situation's meaning, and a combination of both approaches.

Diverting Attention

Engage in a contrary or compensating activity. Imagine you are camping and are afflicted with a toothache. You have no aspirin, and the nearest store is a day's drive away. However unavoidable the pain may be, it can be dealt with. One option is to engage in a mental or real-life activity that is incompatible with the pain. You might fantasize sunning yourself on the beach, having fun at the park, or riding a hot air balloon.

A similar procedure can be applied to other stress situations. Imagine you have a monotonous job, with no prospects of advancement. For example, you might have to spend hours a day driving a truck. Although you are skilled at working with others, in this job you work alone. To deal with this predicament, you might seek out activities outside of work that involve just the opposite of working alone, for example, joining a club or church group. The idea is to involve yourself in activities incompatible with the specific type of frustration associated with work; put differently, select activities that might help compensate for needs that are frustrated.

Focus attention away from the situation. Often it is useful to occupy yourself with some form of activity that diverts your attention from the painful situation. If you are suffering from a toothache, you might busy yourself with cleaning house, watching television, or even planning activities in your mind. You might deal with unavoidable job stress by focusing on certain trivial elements of the job (counting the number of tasks you complete). When possible, take an occasional break in which you can attend to something other than work; for example, relaxation, reading the paper, talking to friends. At the end of the day, or the week, distract yourself with an enjoyable activity such as a movie, dance, or card game.

Changing a Situation's Meaning

Transform the situation. This strategy involves reinterpreting your present situation as something other than pain or discomfort, or relabeling these sensations as minimal. You might imagine your toothache as being soothed or numbed with novocaine, ice water, or the hot sun. You might also imagine changing context; for example, picturing yourself as possessing a mechanical jaw insensitive to pain, or as an injured football player who must continue in spite of the pain. Returning to our truck driving example, you might imagine you are piloting an important cargo ship through space, or avoiding potential threats set up by a fantasized adversary.

Look at the bright side. What good might come from the stressful situation? You might view pain as a challenge, a test of your ability to continue undistracted, or an opportunity to deepen your relaxation skills. Frustrations at work can be viewed as opportunities to develop your ability to tolerate frustration. One way of achieving this is to focus on affirmations of those strengths and abilities you display by tolerating the situation. You might think, "I can take this, I have the endurance, I am increasing my ability to go on, I am growing by pushing myself to the limit."

What meaning can be found? Is there meaning to be found in confronting pain and discomfort? What broader lessons can they teach us about who we are and what life is all about? Often, when all seems hopeless, we have an opportunity to revise basic assumptions as well as deeply held personal philosophies. We can acquire a new ability to see things in perspective. We will return to this important topic in our final chapter.

Combination Approaches

Attend to the situation in a detached manner. This strategy involves not turning away from discomfort, but attempting to attend to it calmly and dispassionately. Simply attend to the toothache, or the frustrating aspects of work. You might attempt to intellectually analyze different aspects of your discomfort, as if you were a scientist or detective making a report. Continue attending until you can do so while maintaining a neutral frame of mind. This strategy contains elements of diverting attention as well as changing the meaning of a situation. By focusing on the situation, you divert attention from catastrophizing worries and thoughts that can make things worse. In addition, you prove to yourself that the pain is indeed bearable.

Look for chances to talk about your feelings. Pain and discomfort can often be tolerated better if we share our feelings with someone we trust. Ideally, the person should be a "good listener." That is, he or she should sincerely care about how we feel, indicate some understanding, and refrain from making judgmental proclamations.

Put it into words or pictures. Sometimes simply attempting to clearly express your feelings of pain and discomfort can help. Such self-expression can take the form of writing in a journal; creating a song, poem, or work of art; or even contemplation or prayer.

11

Out of the Theater and into the World: The Ten-step Path

We have just about completed our exploration of stress scripting. However, we have not considered one very important point. How does one become an "expert" at stress scripting? How does one learn the principles of stress management so well that they become spontaneous, just as a master actor learns to speak his or her lines effortlessly? The answer is simple--practice. Specifically, one becomes a master at stress scripting through three types of practice: paper practice, mental practice, and active practice. Throughout this book we have been engaging in paper practice. Written exercises at the end of this book give you an opportunity to think through what might happen in a stress situation, what you might think and do, and how you might deal with relapse. In this chapter we will consider more thoroughly mental and active practice.

MENTAL PRACTICE

In mental practice you imagine or fantasize yourself encountering and dealing with all phases of a stress situation, pre-stress, mid-stress, and post-stress. Include the following:

1. Cues
2. Irrational and self-defeating thoughts
3. Relaxation
4. Rational and useful thoughts and behavior
5. Completion thoughts

Imagine you could see inside the mind of someone mentally rehearsing a stressful situation. Here is what you might see. In the margin to the left we have indicated what principles are being applied.

The Report

Pre-stress	I work for a local manufacturing firm and at the end of every month we have a staff meeting. My job is to make a report on marketing strategies, a task which creates considerable stress for me. In rehearsing this situation, I think of what happens three or four days before my report, since this is when my stress actually begins.
Cue	Specifically, my stress begins when I look at my calendar and see the circled meeting day. I feel a sinking sensation in my
Irrational, self-defeating thinking	stomach and start thinking, "Oh my God, I don't have enough time to prepare my report. I'm going to be a complete failure. I sure hope John, my arrogant coworker, doesn't interrupt
Relaxation	me." I close my eyes and take ten slow, deep breaths, a relaxation exercise I have learned earlier. When I have calmed
Rational, useful thinking	down somewhat, I think, "I have given this report before. I know what to do. Simply prepare the facts, one by one. If
[DERC script]	John interrupts, I'll simply use a DERC script on him--point out that he is interrupting, that it is distracting, and ask him to let
Completion thought	me continue. There, that was more realistic. I'm getting better.

Mid-stress

Relaxation

Cue

Irrational,
self-defeating thinking

Relaxation

Rational, useful
thinking and behavior
[DERC script]

Completion thought

Post-stress

Irrational,
self-defeating thinking

Cue

Then I imagine the day of the meeting. Our coordinator asked who wanted to give their report first. I wait until last. I close my eyes, take a few breaths, and start reading. In the middle of the report, John interrupts, "Can't you hurry things up. I've got to meet my wife for lunch." Anger starts building in my stomach. I start thinking, "This stupid fool. He only cares about himself." I catch myself and realize that he probably doesn't realize how rude his interruptions are. After taking a deep breath, I reply, "I'm sorry, but I was in the middle of an important point when you interrupted me. This kind of interruption distracts me and gets me off track. Please let me finish without interruption and we will be done in the shortest period of time. I want to get out of here as much as you do." There, that's a reasonable way of dealing with this problem. Good, I can do it. I've finished my plan and am ready to begin.

After the meeting that night, I start thinking about what happened. My first thoughts are, "Boy, I came across as really defensive. Everybody's going to think that I can't take it." I catch myself and think, "Here I go again, putting myself down needlessly. Let's think rational

Rational, useful thinking   ly. I didn't do all that badly. I
                                              remembered to practice my
                                              relaxation exercise--good.   I
Completion thought   didn't explode when interrupted.
                                              And I carefully kept to my
                                              DERC script. However, I did
                                              make a mistake waiting until
                                              last.   My anxiety level just
                                              increased. Next time, I'll vol-
                                              unteer to be first. I've done all
                                              I can. Its time to go on.

Here is another example of a fantasized stress situation. See if you
can identify the stress concepts and steps we have just discussed.

The Date

I have my first date with Joan next week. I start feeling upset the
day before, so that is where my coping fantasy begins. I imagine
myself alone at home. I turn off the TV and start thinking about my
date. My mind begins to think about all the possible things that
could go wrong. Suddenly, I realize what I have done. It is best
to keep busy the night before. It's just not a good idea to be idle--
my mind goes wild. So the moment I notice I'm not doing
anything, I catch myself, relax, and think, "Wait a minute. Keep
busy. You've done everything you can to prepare. Why not read
a book?"

I am now on my date with Joan. We are discussing the day over
dinner. Unexpectedly, we run out of things to say. Neither of us
says a thing for an uncomfortable period of time. My heart begins
to beat quickly. I start thinking, "Gosh, she must think I'm stupid.
I'm a complete dolt." Then I let go and think, "Now wait a minute.
There is nothing wrong with a little silence. Perhaps she's as
uncomfortable as I am. This is the time I can ask about what's
she's thinking and feeling." I say, "We've been quiet a little while.
May I ask what you're thinking?" Good. That wasn't so hard.

My date is over. The next day I think about what happened. I sure
enjoyed some of the time, but things got a little boring during
dinner. I really should be able to keep someone entertained every
minute. Now, wait a minute, relax. That's not logical. I'm not a
performer on stage during a date. Just be myself, and that's good

enough. And I did a fine job handling the silence. There, that's a better way of thinking.

It is very useful to rehearse how you might handle failures and setbacks. The same steps we have just discussed are involved; however the stress situation changes to dealing with relapse. Let's take the example we started with:

The Report: Dealing with Setback

I am to give an important report at a business meeting. For weeks I have been working on it. I am sitting with my coworkers at a large conference table and the meeting begins. Our coordinator asks who wants to give their report first. I wait until last. When my turn is up, I close my eyes, take a few breaths, and start reading. In the middle of the report, one committee member, John, interrupts, "Can't you hurry things up. I've got to meet my wife for lunch." Anger starts building in my stomach. This is a disaster. Why did John have to come to the meeting? I start thinking, "This stupid fool. He only cares about himself. He's going to ruin everything for me."

I catch myself, relax, and realize that he probably doesn't realize how rude his interruptions are. I slowly turn to John and reply, "I'm sorry, but I was in the middle of an important point when you interrupted me. This kind of interruption distracts me and gets me off track. Please let me finish without interruption and we will be done in the shortest period of time. I want to get out of here as much as you do." John interrupts again, "I think you have made your point. Let's go on with the meeting." I find myself getting very angry and just about slam the table with my fist. The situation is getting too much for me. I am afraid my coping plan isn't working. I think, "Oh no, this is the end of the world."

I then remember my fall-back strategy. I discretely close and open my eyes, take a deep breath, and read the rest of my main points. My decision is to ignore John for the moment. When my report is finished, I turn to John and say, "There is something I would like to talk to you about later today. I'll give you a ring." There, that's a reasonable way of dealing with this setback. I finish my report. My anger is so intense that it would be counterproductive to attempt to be assertive with John. So I decide to deal with him later, when I am ready. Not bad.

Finally, even those unfortunate situations of unavoidable pain and discomfort can be effectively rehearsed.   The following patient is recovering from a severe burn wound.   At times the pain from skin grafts to her hand seems unbearable.   In anticipation of such moments, she practices the following fantasy.

The Pain

A few months ago I injured my hand.   Although it has healed, I still feel pain.   My pain usually starts with a tingling sensation in my hand and grows to a point of high intensity.   My hand feels like it is burning up.   When the tingling begins, I sometimes start to clench up and panic.   I start thinking, "Here it comes; I can't take it."   I wonder if I am going to go crazy with the pain.   Then I catch myself.   "Tingling.   That's my signal to apply pain management. One step at a time.   I can do it."

I close my eyes and begin focusing on my meditation image, a cool iceberg in the arctic.   Whenever my mind wanders, I gently bring it back to this image.   After five minutes, I focus on my injured hand.   I let myself feel the pain, imagining it is the intense cold caused by ice touching my skin.   I let this phrase calmly repeat in my mind, "Cooling ice.   The sensation is intense, but OK.   I am calmed and refreshed.   With every outgoing breath, heat and tension flow away.   My mind and pain cool off."   I take a deep breath and sigh.   "Good, I have the ability to deal with pain."

ACTIVE PRACTICE

There are three types of active practice: role-playing, situational setups, and real-life.   Role playing involves play-acting a stress situation with a friend, stress-management group, or therapist.   Two or more people act out the situation, and any others serve as "reviewers," who observe and provide feedback.   It is important to replay roles, over and over, incorporating feedback each time.   Once again, attempt graduated versions.

Role-playing has a number of advantages over real-life practice. Since you are simulating the real world, you can practice and try out various solutions in a safe environment.   You can get other ideas on coping options and perfect your skills.

Here are several role-playing scenarios.

Voicing Thoughts

This exercise contains elements of mental and active practice. After defining your stress situation, say out loud your thought lines. Then you and others can decide which are self-defeating and irrational, and which are useful and rational.

Direct Role-Playing

Direct role-playing is the simplest form of play-acting a script. Select another person to role play with you. You play yourself, and the other person plays the other person in your script. Both of you begin by reading through the script to get an idea of what each person says and does. When you are ready, act out the entire script.

Switching Roles

Once again, select another person to role play with you. However, this time your partner plays your part, reading your script, while you play the person to whom the script is directed. By switching roles, you can anticipate unexpected reactions to your script, and your partner can help evaluate its effectiveness.

Advisor Role-Playing

Here you need at least two additional players, someone to whom you are relating, and someone to sit or stand next to you as an advisor. When you are play-acting your script (using either direct role-playing or switched roles), your advisor has the option of whispering suggestions to you as to what to say and do.

Playing the Observer

At times, it is more effective to simply select other people to play the parts in your stress situation. You select who plays you and the other person. Provide guidelines as to what they should say. Then observe their performance. Often playing the observer provides you with the opportunity to objectively see your script in a new light.

Once you have finished role playing, obtain feedback on your performance. Use the following questions as guidelines. Then replay the situation, incorporating your feedback. Often it is best to attempt to improve one aspect of your performance at a time. First improve your goal-directed behavior. Then polish up the extent to which you stuck to the facts. In step-by-step fashion consider all of the following questions.

1. What were your problem-solving and self-expression goals? How well were they achieved?
2. Did you stick to the SCRIPT rules?
3. What stress thoughts might interfere with the successful completion of this script? What are some rational and useful alternatives?
4. To what extent did your nonverbal behavior add to the effectiveness of your script?
5. Can you think of ways the other person might reasonably attempt to deviate from your script? How might you counter this?

In a situational setup you deliberately seek out a stress situation you know you can deal with. Do not overwhelm yourself with an excessively threatening situation. Simply pick one that has relatively few consequences for you. For example, if you are working on shyness at parties, deliberately walk up to a stranger and attempt to maintain a conversation for five minutes.

In a real-life stress encounter, you attempt to deal with a stress situation which you had little choice but to encounter. It is through such unplanned encounters that we have a chance to see our stress skills in action, and determine which need to be perfected. Also, real-life encounters provide an excellent opportunity for dealing with post-stress reactions. Here you can reward yourself for what went well, and review what you might do better.

THE TEN-STEP PATH

We have encountered one idea again and again throughout this program: in learning to manage stress it is important to take gradual steps. Rather than begin with the most difficult and dramatic problems, start with the easy ones, evaluate your progress, reward yourself, and then move on.

So far we have been taking steps by working with progressively more complex coping strategies. First we simply learned to analyze a stress situation into various script components--Behavior Lines, Speech Lines, Thought Lines, and Feeling Lines. We then differentiated coping from defense, eventually considering assertiveness, non-assertiveness, and aggressiveness. Next we learned to differentiate various forms of self-defeating and irrational stress thinking. Eventually we learned to go beyond simple assertiveness with complex assertiveness scripts that anticipate the defensive sabotaging reactions of others.

The *ten-step path* gives you an opportunity to put all of your skills together. The path is actually a series of progressively difficult coping tasks you set out to accomplish under the supervision of a qualified mental health professional. The first step is select a problem stress situation, using the SCRIPT rules. Make sure your problem is simple, concrete, realistic, important, personal, and timely. For example, you might select "Talking to the boss about my wishes and ideas about the work environment." Next, construct a *stress hierarchy*, a list of different versions of your stress situation, ranked from easiest to most difficult (or most stressful). In your hierarchy, include three situations in which you might encounter a coping relapse or setback. For example, describe situations in which you might engage in self-sabotage after you have started to cope. Or describe sabotaging efforts of others. Here's a sample hierarchy (including three relapse situations):

1. The boss laughs at me when I ask for a raise (relapse situation).
2. I ask the boss for a raise.
3. I receive a critical evaluation from the boss.
4. I forget my script before asking for a raise (relapse situation).
5. I criticize the boss.
6. I ask for a different office, but am ignored (relapse situation).
7. Asking the boss for a change of office.
8. Giving an important report to the boss.
9. Asking the boss for advice concerning an important report.
10. Sitting with boss at lunch engaging in small talk.

You can use your stress hierarchy as a map or path that defines how far you want to proceed in practicing your stress management skills. Here's how. Start with your easiest situation; ignore for now those that are more difficult. Once you can successfully complete three mental practice sessions, one role-play practice session, and one active practice session, you can consider this situation reasonably mastered, and proceed to the next most difficult situation.

Finally, it is important to emphasize the importance of proceeding on this path under the supervision of a qualified mental health professional, that is, a licensed psychologist, clinical social worker, or psychiatrist. The reason is to assist you in selecting objectives (especially active practice) that are within your grasp and have a reasonably low possibility of backfiring. In addition, it is useful to have a qualified professional help you deal with unexpected problems that might arise. If you have decided to proceed without professional assistance, I recommend completing only the *mental practice* components of the stress path.

12

Beyond Scripting

I have a friend who seems to deal with stress particularly well. I always wanted to know his secret technique. One day I asked him, and his answer surprised me. Instead of describing a special exercise or strategy, he said:

After a stressful work situation, I sit back and put things in perspective. In the final analysis, how important are my many work problems and hassles to me? At work, no matter how stressful, I am acting out certain roles, nothing more. I play my part. The play can go well or poorly, but it is still a play. And when my day is over, the curtain falls on the various soap operas of the job. I return home to what really matters--my family, my friends, my church, and so on. My relationships with others are the most important thing in life. I take part in the play of work to put food on the table and to provide the resources to live and share with the other people in my life.

What is interesting is that my friend did not describe a specific set of coping strategies. Instead, he shared his thoughts concerning stress. But his thinking represents more than rational or useful thoughts. Indeed, it goes beyond a problem-solving or negotiating attitude. What we see is evidence of a basic and encompassing personal philosophy. In this chapter we will see that such philosophies often provide the ultimate key to dealing with stress. To understand, we need to begin with situations where the strategies we have outlined in this book are just not enough.

Most books on stress and assertiveness begin with an affirmation of "assertiveness rights" (the right to say "no," express your feelings, and so on). However, these books usually leave unanswered a very basic question--What do you do when rights are in conflict? To understand, let's examine this script:

> SITUATION: Two friends have asked a favor of John. Sue has known John a long time and would like him to help her move on Friday. George is a relatively new friend who would like a drive to the airport the same day of
> Sue's move. Either request represents something of an inconvenience, since John had planned to study for an upcoming college exam the day of the requests.
> THOUGHT LINE: "Should I help out one of my friends this day? I have the right to decline a friend's request if I really want to. But if I decide to help, should I help Sue because I have known her a long time? Or does our long-standing relationship give me the right to decline? Should I help George? We are good friends, and I haven't really helped him out before at all. What should I do?"

Clearly, John has a conflict. The coping tools presented so far simply do not help. Now, let's examine an internal dialogue I recently had while practicing relaxation. I began relaxing, and began to think "I should be spending my time planning for this important interview tomorrow. I would really like to have this settled; what gives me the right to take this half hour off?"

Obviously, all of us have the right to cope, to defend ourselves, and to relax. But simply affirming such rights, and acquiring the skills to put them into action, does not solve the dilemma of how to make difficult choices. Life is, of course, filled with such choices. Should you assertively confront a friend concerning his lack of faithfulness to his wife? Or does your friendship require that you keep your nose out of his personal business? Should you quit meditation because one month of practice has not yielded the results you have desired? It would be more fun to spend time playing more tennis with a friend. Or should you continue with a somewhat boring and frustrating exercise until you begin to develop relaxation skills?

Questions like these are more easily answered when we have a guiding philosophy to live and act by. If you believe that "A good friend must be willing to talk about anything, even moral issues," then you have guidance on whether to confront your friend. Similarly, if you believe that "A good friend respects differences in moral standards," this philosophy too can help you.

Personal philosophies serve many uses. The serve as quick reminders of the coping or relaxation paths we have chosen and inform us when action is or is not called for. They help guide our choices when we are confused. They give us courage to act, even when we may feel too comfortable, depressed, anxious, or irritated to do so. They tell us when sacrifice is needed, and when it is not. In sum, our personal philosophies give us a reason to cope assertively, and a reason to explore the depths of relaxation. And they give us a reason to persevere in the face of possible relapse. These points I have introduced elsewhere (Smith, 1987, 1990, in press) and are worth elaborating here.

A personal philosophy must answer at least three basic questions: What do I believe in? What do I value? What are my commitments? Our beliefs consist of our enduring thoughts about what is real and factual. What are the facts concerning ourselves, others, and the world? Examples include:

"The earth travels around the sun."
"Smoking is unhealthy."
"Assertive people have less stress."
"Relaxation reduces stress and tension."

Our values consist of what we think is important. For example:

"I want to live a long and healthy life."
"Friends are important to me."
"I want to be successful at work."
"I value doing my best."

Finally, our commitments represent what actions we have chosen to take. Examples include:

"I have decided to read and try this stress management book."
"I am committed to reducing my weight by cutting down on fats in my diet."
"I have decided to give generously to my church."
"I will spend at least one day a week with my family."

Obviously, all beliefs, values, and commitments are not equally important. We will consider a special kind of personal philosophy, the *coping philosophy*, which consists of enduring beliefs, values, and commitments relevant to stress and coping. Such a philosophy must include your basic thoughts concerning action as well as relaxation. Here are the beliefs, values, and commitments of one coping philosophy.

Healthy Action and Rest

Coping beliefs. Assertive and realistic coping is good for my health. Undue hostility and passivity simply increases inner tension. The ability to deeply relax is also healthy, and can help me prevent and recover from unnecessary tension.

Coping values. My health is important to me. After all, if I lose my health, what do I have left?

Coping commitments. In addition to exercising and eating right, I will try to deal with stress assertively and think about stress in practical, realistic terms. I will practice my relaxation exercises daily.

Coping philosophies can be rather narrowly defined, like the one above, or more encompassing. Here are some additional, somewhat more broadly defined coping philosophies.

Living and Relaxing in the Present

Coping beliefs. The past is history, water under the bridge. What has happened before no longer has to affect me. Similarly, the future has not yet happened. What hasn't happened can't affect me. The only reality is the present moment.

Coping values. My present feelings are important. When I am upset, I should do something about it rather than wait for things to get better on their own. When my mind is quiet and relaxed, this too is important. The present moment matters.

Coping commitments. Live one day at a time. Live in the present. Put aside worries about past and future. When relaxing, put aside all thoughts and plans and simply attend to the present. When becoming involved in the world, express your present feelings in a realistic and effective way.

Taking Feelings Seriously

Coping beliefs. People sometimes try to tell me what I should be feeling. They might say, "You're not really feeling upset," "You're just confused about who you are," "Your anger is just a passing phase."

Even when I talk about relaxation experiences that seem really deep, they might say, "You have only hypnotized yourself. It's nothing, just a daydream." I have learned to treat my feelings as real. They are very much a part of who I am.

Coping values. Furthermore, what I feel is important to me. I take my feelings seriously. If I am depressed or angry, that's an important feeling. Something is wrong. When I am in a deeply relaxed and dreamy state, that too is important. I trust and value what I feel.

Coping commitments. I chose to do something about my feelings. I tell people what's on my mind. I practice relaxation regularly to keep in touch with that important part of me.

Love and Sharing

Coping beliefs. I believe that it is love and sharing that keeps people together. Through love and sharing I can come in contact with what is real in others, and let them encounter the real me. It is love that provides the energy of life that enables us to cope and grow.

Coping values. I value love above all else. This includes love for myself and love for others.

Coping commitments. I try to live my life by sharing my love with others. In addition, when I hurt or am troubled, I try to see if I am doing unloving things toward myself. Even spending time with myself in quiet meditation is an act of love. I calmly accept all that comes to mind, even upsetting thoughts and feelings. I lovingly accept what my mind has to offer, just as a mother accepts her child.

Achieving My Potential

Coping beliefs. I believe I have untapped skills and abilities. Furthermore, I believe that actualizing skills and abilities contributes to human fulfillment.

Coping values. I value reaching my potential, even if this means giving up short-term comfort and satisfaction for long-term gain.

Coping commitments. I make a point of devoting some time each week to developing one of my skills. I take risks when it is clear that risk-taking may be a way out of stagnation and contribute to growth.

We can now see how coping philosophies can work. Notice how the examples above help provide answers to some of the following common life dilemmas.

I guess I am a workaholic, a very driven person. Last night I was pressing myself to complete all the work I could possibly do. I then sat back, and realized, "This is silly. My health comes first. Being a compulsive workaholic and perfectionist isn't helping my high blood pressure one bit. I will take the entire evening off for a healthy rest."

I've been dating Jan for over a month. However, it just isn't working. I feel really uncomfortable telling her that I think we should stop dating. Part of me says that I have the right to simply drop out of sight for a few weeks. That would certainly be the comfortable thing for me to do. Another part of me says, "Be assertive." I finally decided that love and caring for others is really important to me. For her sake, I should put aside feelings of discomfort I might have, and let her know how I feel. And by telling her my true feelings, I am taking them very seriously, serious enough to take a risk in sharing them with others.

I've just had heart surgery and the doctor has told me to avoid excess stress for the next two weeks. My heart needs time to recover. I find myself beginning to worry about the real risks I face. In fact, I might experience complications. It is true that some people die from heart surgery. I then catch myself. This worry, although possibly realistic, is not good for me. Right now, my most important task is to survive. I'll let myself pretend that everything is going to be OK. Worry is taboo. I'm a very healthy person. I'm going to avoid all possibly troublesome encounters. Let the doctor worry about my problems. I'll deal with them when she say's I'm ready.

Last week my friend was 20 or 30 minutes late for an important meeting. Part of me wanted to raise my voice and express my anger, even if her feelings might be hurt. Another part of me wanted to carefully point out how her lateness inconvenienced me and created considerable irritation. I feel I have the right to ventilate intense feelings, but I also have the right to moderate my feelings and present the objective facts of a problem situation. Basically I see myself as a problem solver, one who tries to come up with the best solution for everyone. With that in mind, I said, "We have a problem. You are 20 minutes late. Frankly, I have the urge to let my anger out. But I also want to find out what happened, and try to figure out how we can avoid this problem in the future."

Many people haven't thought through a coping philosophy. Doing so involves asking the three basic questions we have been discussing. What are your answers?

Belief Questions: "What is basically real and true about myself, others, and the world?"

"I am capable of learning to cope better."
"Ineffective coping creates stress."
"Relaxation reduces unhealthy tension."
"Only I can help myself."
"I have only one life to live; I want to make the best of it while I can."
"God has a plan for my life."
"My worries and concerns are the result of how I distort what I see."
"I am capable of solving problems."
"I can be reasonably happy in spite of my burdens."
"Even pain can be a source of wisdom and insight."

Value Questions: "What is most important to me? For what would I be willing to sacrifice time and effort?"

"My health comes first."
"Loving and caring for others is most important to me."
"I value growing to reach my potential."
"God's plan is the center of my life."
"My materialistic possessions are not the most important things in life."
"I value those things in life that are beautiful."
"Some things are even more important than my deepest miseries."

Commitment Questions: "What am I willing to do in light of my beliefs and values? How am I willing to sacrifice time and effort?"

"I will devote 30 minutes a day to practicing relaxation."
"When I feel something strongly concerning another person, I will share this feeling if appropriate."
"I will take some risks in being assertive."
"Even if my anxious worries seem true, I will examine them to see if they are self-defeating or irrational."
"God's will be done."
"I choose to treat stress as a problem-to-be-solved."

CONFRONTING, LETTING GO, AND RISKING

In most general terms, a coping philosophy helps us attend to and confront problems we might be tempted to avoid. It helps us let go of that which cannot be changed. And, most important, it can give us the courage to take risks, to experiment even when the results are uncertain or hard to predict. These are three philosophical dimensions of all coping--confronting, letting go, and risking. Even the simplest act of relaxing, whether it be on a yoga stretch or a meditation, requires attending to the task at hand. And to relax, one must let go of the urge to plan ahead, worry, and so on--one simply relaxes. And finally the student of relaxation must be open to potentially unexpected experiences, deep levels of rest perhaps never encountered before. In relaxation, the dimensions of coping become focusing, passivity, and receptivity.

Assertiveness, as well as rational and useful thinking, involve the dimensions of coping even more directly. When we contract to be assertive, we confront and let go of our non-assertiveness or aggressiveness, and risk acting on our honest feelings and thoughts. When we decide to think in ways conducive to coping, we first confront and let go of our self-defeating and irrational thought patterns and, then again, risk thinking in new ways.

Most fundamentally, your coping philosophy guides you to face reality, to let go when that is called for, and to be open to change. As such, a coping philosophy is much more than a script. It is something of a map that points to a more rewarding life. In once sense, life may well be a play, and all of us actors. In a deeper sense it is a path and we are explorers. Let me end with a thought adapted from a book I wrote on relaxation (Smith, 1989):

> The promise of relaxation, and of coping, is always there, silently waiting to be discovered. When tension is calmed, often something of lesser importance is set aside. A source of noise is stilled. And we can see with clearer perspective and act with greater honesty and freedom. By letting go of what is truly expendable, it is easier to find what really matters.

Part 3

A Relaxation Supplement

Lesson 1

What Is Relaxation?

Relaxation training is an important part of stress management. However, different approaches work for different people. You, or your stress management trainer or therapist, may already have an approach. If so, fine. Simply use it whenever this book indicates. If you have not been trained in relaxation, or wish to increase your relaxation skill, you may want to try the approach presented in this section.

The type of relaxation we will explore first involves learning five basic approaches--isometric squeeze relaxation (or "progressive relaxation"), yogaform stretching, breathing, thematic imagery, and meditation. Next, you develop an individualized program consisting of those exercises that work best for you. Finally, you abbreviate and streamline exercises for use outside of the practice session.

Before we continue, it is important to consider some general goals of all relaxation. First of all, relaxation must help reduce unhealthy and unproductive levels of tension. To elaborate, each of us has a built-in stress energy "fight or flight" response. As we have seen earlier, our bodies can automatically, without planning, prepare for vigorous, emergency action. Your heart pumps hard. You breathe more rapidly. Your muscles become tense. In all, hundreds of changes take place as your adrenalin flows. The stress energy response is absolutely essential for survival. It provides the football player with that needed shot of energy to make a touchdown, and you the energy to run from the neighborhood dog. However, this fight or flight response can also be triggered by events that are not life-threatening such as worry, everyday hassles, even the alarm clock.

The result is that many of us experience unhealthy levels of stress, a problem that can contribute to a variety of illnesses, as well as reduced work productivity and ability to enjoy life.

Often deep relaxation can help counter excessive levels of stress energy. However, such relaxation is not achieved through watching television, reading books, or drinking a beer. Special training and practice is usually required. Once achieved, skill at deep relaxation can enable one to evoke a healthful and restorative "relaxation response," a reduction in heart rate, breathing, and muscle tension that is the opposite of the stress response.

Relaxation training is not over once you have mastered the relaxation response. This goal is only the beginning. Central to all relaxation is the acquisition of three basic mental skills--focusing, passivity, and receptivity. Let's take three examples:

One day I was doing my housework. Everything was happening at once--the TV was on, the kids were playing outside, the upstairs neighbors were playing loud music, and so on. I was getting very tense and decided I needed a rest. I went to my quiet den, closed the door, took the phone off the hook, and told myself "for the next few minutes I'm going ignore all the distractions and attend to one thing--reading my favorite magazine."

I was getting really tense over my job. Everything seemed like it had to be done at once. I was being pulled in a hundred directions at once, first to answer the phone, then work on a report, then answer a letter. Finally I said to myself "Look, take it easy. Relax. Do one thing at a time and let everything else be."

After studying a few hours I like to rest on my couch and close my eyes. I let a pleasant fantasy of some distant tropical island go through my mind. One day, I began to feel like I was floating. This was a new and strange sensation and I almost got up and called the doctor. However, I then decided that these feelings are OK, just a sign that I am relaxing. Now I even pretend I am floating when I'm relaxing.

The person who thinks, "I'm going to ignore all the distractions" has, in a simple way, decided to focus, that is, to quietly attend to a restricted stimulus. In the second example, the statement, "Do one thing at a time" represents a decision to let go of unnecessary striving and take a more passive stance toward the world. Finally, the student who realizes that his sensations of floating are "OK, just a sign that I am relaxing," has learned to be more receptive and tolerate experiences that may at first seem uncertain, unfamiliar, or paradoxical.

We can now define relaxation skills more formally. *Focusing* is the ability to attend to a simple stimulus for an extended period of time; *passivity*, the ability to stop unnecessary goal-directed and analytic activity; and *receptivity*, the ability to tolerate and accept experiences that may be uncertain, unfamiliar, or paradoxical. These basic skills are what makes all relaxation work. Indeed, they are essential to all effective and rewarding activity. The ballet dancer must above all focus on the movements of the dance, not the crowd, yesterday's problems, and the like. The effective business manager must know how to put aside needless worry and preoccupation with trivia; he or she must be able to display a stance of passivity or "letting be" concerning these issues. The innovator, whether it be artist or entrepreneur, must be receptive to the new and unexpected.

Successful practitioners of all forms of relaxation, whether it be yoga, zen, prayer, or muscle relaxation, are essentially doing the same thing--honing and refining their ability to attend to a limited stimulus; ceasing unnecessary goal-directed and analytic striving; and tolerating and accepting experiences that may be uncertain, unfamiliar, and paradoxical. What distinguishes the master from the beginner is not alpha brain wave activity, reduced heart rate, and so on (indeed, there may well be no differences in arousal), but the degree of focusing, passivity, and receptivity they can display. But there is even more to relaxation than skill mastery.

Perhaps the most important characteristic of truly deep relaxation is the relaxer's personal philosophies--enduring thoughts about what is real, important, and worthy of action. For example, if you firmly believe that the most important thing in life is to drive yourself and be perfect in all things, it is easy to see how you might have trouble learning a relaxation discipline. Conversely, the belief "live one day at a time, do not concern yourself over that which cannot be changed" is much more conducive to relaxation. I have found that there are hundreds of thought structures that can interfere with relaxation, including:

"I am not capable of making my life better."
"Things will automatically get better on their own."
"I do not feel good about myself when I am less than totally

successful at work or school."
"Unless others love and accept me, I can't feel at peace with myself."

Unless a relaxer can learn to relinquish such beliefs, he or she will go nowhere with relaxation. However, perhaps the deepest task of relaxation is developing personal philosophies more conducive to relaxation. Some of these philosophies include:

"My selfish worries are distractions that fog awareness of a deeper reality."
"The meaning of life becomes more apparent to me in the quiet of relaxation."
"Live one day at a time."
"First things first."
"My urgent concerns seem less important when seen in broader perspective."
"There are more important things than my everyday hassles."
"At the deepest level I can feel at peace with myself--I am an OK person."
"God's will be done."

A person is deeply relaxed when he or she has truly learned to focus and maintain a stance of passivity and receptivity. Relaxation is even more profound when special supportive personal philosophies are acquired.

Given these goals--learning the relaxation response, relaxation skills, and relaxation personal philosophies--what is the best way to go about learning relaxation? We will be using a new approach called *cognitive-behavioral relaxation training* (Smith, 1989, 1990). This approach is based on the assumption that different types of relaxation have different effects and work for different people. Because of this, we will try a variety of approaches and select those exercises that work best for a personalized relaxation program. We will conclude by learning how to streamline and abbreviate relaxation so it can be used in special circumstances.

Before beginning relaxation training, it is essential to make sure you are ready. Below is a relaxation "Start Off Checklist" that covers some of the preliminaries (Smith, 1989).

Have you selected practice times during which you are relatively unlikely to be distracted? Remember: it is not a good idea to practice when you have some other duty that has to be done.

Do you have a comfortable relaxation chair?

Do you have a quiet place in which to practice? If you are going to practice in a place where there are other people, try to make sure you won't be interrupted. You might want to close the door to your room. Ask friends or family members not to interrupt while you are "resting." And it's OK to take the phone off the hook.

You should not take a nonprescription drug (e.g., marijuana, amphetamines, barbiturates, psychedelic drugs) or alcohol for at least a day before practicing. Such drugs can make it more difficult to relax or focus attention on what you are doing. At the very least, they can limit the extent to which the effects of relaxation will generalize outside the session.

You should not have a drink containing caffeine (coffee, tea, cola) for at least 2 hours before practicing. Caffeine can make it more difficult to relax and focus attention on what you are doing.

You should not smoke tobacco for at least an hour before practicing.

You should not eat any food for at least an hour before practicing. If you are absolutely starving, eat a carrot.

When you are finished, come out of relaxation very slowly and gently. Arising too abruptly can be jarring and even make you feel dizzy. Take about 60 seconds to easily open your eyes all the way. Then stretch your arms to your sides and take a deep breath.

Finally, here are some general precautions that apply to all relaxation (Smith, 1989, pp. 23-24).

Learning relaxation is like learning any other skill, whether it be swimming, driving a car, or singing: you have to start with the basics and build up; you have to practice; and you have to be patient. To ensure maximum benefit, you should practice your techniques twice daily, 20-30 minutes a session. Moderate benefits can be obtained by practicing once a day. Less frequent practice can be useful for those who are not interested in mastering the skill of self-relaxation, but desire a simple demonstration of specific techniques.

Don't expect immediate results, as few skills are mastered overnight. Often the effects are gradual. And different exercises will work for different people. Some exercises in this program simply may not be the right ones for you.

One important piece of advice applies to every exercise presented in this program. If an exercise makes you uncomfortable in any way, first try shortening it (doing it for 15 minutes instead of 25) and exerting less effort. If it still makes you uncomfortable, drop the exercise unless you are under professional supervision. This advice is so important that it merits repeating: if an exercise hurts, makes you dizzy, anxious, or depressed, or feels unpleasant or uncomfortable in any way, ease up and spend less time at it. If the problem continues, stop the exercise, unless you are under professional supervision.

On rare occasions relaxation exercises can have unwanted physical effects. While for most people self-relaxation is comfortable and safe, seek medical permission before beginning training if you now or have had in the past any of the following conditions:

Backaches
Blackouts
Cerebro-vascular accident
Depression (severe)
Diabetes
Glaucoma
Heart disease
Hypoglycemia
Hypertension
Pregnancy (third trimester)
Thyroid disorder
Transient ischemic attacks
Any recent or serious disorder affecting bones, ligaments, or
    muscles.

Most relaxation training manuals, including this one, warns that relaxation training can alter the required dosage levels for prescription medication, particularly for patients undergoing treatment for hypertension, diabetes, depression, anxiety, and any disorder influenced by changes in general metabolic rate. Although the potential for risk has not bee consistently demonstrated, the state of relaxation itself is frequently associated with changes in general metabolic rate. As a result, need for medication may decrease (and in a few paradoxical cases temporarily increase).

Lesson 2

Isometric Squeeze Relaxation

Our first approach to relaxation is one of the most widely used in America. Isometric squeeze relaxation (also known as "progressive relaxation") is based on a very simple and powerful idea: in order to relax our muscles, it can be useful to first tense up, and then let go. Think of all the times in life you already do this. Have you ever shrugged your shoulders to wring out tension? Even massage, in which someone else squeezes and lets go of your muscles for you, is not unlike isometric squeeze relaxation. However, we will be systematically relaxing all major muscle groups to achieve a relatively deep level of relaxation.

How does isometric squeeze relaxation work? First, prior tensing up can help you learn to differentiate tension from relaxation. Most people under stress have difficulty telling the difference. If you can't tell when you're tense, it's unlikely you'll know when or how to relax. Also, initially tensing up can set into motion a relaxation rebound that actually makes your muscles more relaxed than if you simply tried to "will" them to relax without tensing first. This rebound effect is something like what happens when we shoot an arrow into the air. First we pull the bow string back, creating tension. Then we let go, and the arrow flies into the air. By first tensing up the bow, we are able to shoot the arrow further than if we simply tossed it into the sky.

Isometric squeeze relaxation involves another technique that may seem a bit unusual to you. In every exercise you will have a chance to sooth your muscles by talking to them in a relaxed way. Nearly everyone has spoken a few calming words to an upset baby, or a tense dog or cat. Such soothing talk is not meant to be understood--a baby or pet surely does not know what you are saying. The talk is simply meant to be relaxing.

In a similar way we can silently talk to our muscles. Simply say a few words like "There, there . . . let the tension go. There's nothing you have to do. Simply let go." The goal is not to mechanically repeat such words as a chant, or order your muscles to relax (RELAX, MUSCLES!), but to let your mind passively dwell on a few calming phrases. By doing this, you have little time to think of tension.

Before beginning, try to decide what kinds of soothing muscle self-talk fits you. Once again, the goal is not to effortfully memorize phrases, but quietly let them float through your mind. There are at least 230 very powerful relaxing words you might consider (Smith, 1990). Below is a catalogue of those words hundreds of students and clients have found to be the most effective.

Some Relaxing Words

Absorbed	Composed	Floating	Letting go	Restored
At ease	Concentrated	Flowing	Loose	Safe
Aware	Conscious	Focused	Meditative	Serene
Balanced	Contented	Free	Mellow	Smooth
Calm	Deep	Gentle	Peaceful	Soothed
Carefree	Dreamy	Healthy	Pleasant	Tingling
Centered	Drowsy	In control	Quiet	Tranquil
Cleansed	Easy	In harmony	Refreshed	Unhurried
Clear	Far away	Invigorated	Relaxed	Unworried
Comfortable	Flexible	Laid back	Rested	Warm

You can weave these words into a variety of soothing self-talk phrases, for example:

"Let yourself feel calm."
"Become more and more contented."
"Your cares and concerns feel far away."
"Let feelings of tension flow."
"Become more and more focused."
"As you relax, you still remain in control."
"It's OK to simply let go."
"Let your mind become quiet."
"Feel the warm and tingling sensations that go with relaxation."

Note that these phrases are gentle suggestions, not absolute commands. It is important to avoid making difficult demands on yourself. If you thought, "Become completely relaxed, completely relaxed; let all of your tensions go away," you may create tension. Why? Few people can become *completely* relaxed in a single session or let *all* of their tension flow away. Such demands can create needless tension and worry. Phrase your suggestions in a way that is easy and accepting. For example, you might think, "It's OK to begin to relax and let your tensions begin to go away."

The procedure for isometric squeeze relaxation involves five simple steps:

1. Tense up one muscle group, keeping the rest of the body relaxed. Create a nice good squeeze. Hold the tension for about five seconds.
2. Let go.
3. Pause--for about five to ten seconds simply attend to the sensations that go with relaxation. There is nothing for you to do but enjoy the feelings you have created, and the difference between relaxation and tension.
4. As you let go, passively and effortlessly think three or four relaxation phrases, almost as if you were trying to sooth your muscles by talking to them. Take your time. Talk very slowly, pausing about five to ten seconds between each phrase. Imagine you have a loved pet or child on your lap and you are trying to quiet their tension.
5. Repeat steps 1-4 before moving on.

Here is your entire script for Isometric Squeeze Relaxation.

Isometric Squeeze Relaxation Script

Shoulder Squeeze

1. First attend to your shoulders. While keeping the rest of your body relaxed, shrug. Create a good, complete squeeze. Don't squeeze so much that it hurts, just create a good squeeze. Do this now.
2. Then, *let go*.
3. Pause--notice the feelings of relaxation you can create.
4. Begin your slow, soothing muscle talk.
5. Repeat the cycle.

Back of Neck Squeeze

1. Attend to the muscles in the back of your neck. Squeeze them by gently tilting your head back. Keep the rest of your body relaxed. Create a nice, good squeeze.
2. *Let go.*
3. Pause--enjoy the feelings of relaxation.
4. Begin your slow, soothing muscle talk.
5. Repeat the cycle.

Face Squeeze

1. Attend to the muscles in your face. Make an ugly face by squeezing them all together. Press your lips together, bite hard, push your tongue up, and squint your eyes closed, *now.*
2. *Let go.*
3. Pause--notice the difference between tension and relaxation.
4. Begin your slow, soothing muscle talk.
5. Repeat the cycle.

Front of Neck Squeeze

1. Attend to the muscles of the front of your neck. While keeping the rest of your body relaxed, press your chin down to your chest. Tighten up the muscles in the front of your neck, *now.*
2. *Let go.*
3. Pause--there is nothing for you to do but quietly attend to the feelings of relaxation.
4. Begin your slow, soothing muscle talk.
5. Repeat the cycle.

Back Squeeze

1. Squeeze your back muscles in whatever way feels comfortable. You might just tighten them up. Or press your back against the back of the chair, as if rubbing an itch. Do this now, creating a good squeeze.
2. *Let go.*
3. Pause--compare the feelings of tension and relaxation.
4. Begin your slow, soothing muscle talk.
5. Repeat the cycle.

Stomach and Chest Squeeze

1. Make your stomach muscles hard. You might pull them in, push them out, or simply tighten them up. Do this *now*.
2. *Let go.*
3. Pause--simply attend to the feelings of sinking deeper and deeper into relaxation.
4. Begin your slow, soothing muscle talk.
5. Repeat the cycle.

Right Arm and Side Squeeze

1. Rest both hands comfortably in your lap. In this exercise you are going to squeeze your right arm against your right side (the side of your chest). Imagine you are holding a sponge in your right armpit. Do this *now*.
2. *Let go.*
3. Pause--notice the feelings of relaxation you can create.
4. Begin your slow, soothing muscle talk.
5. Repeat the cycle.

Left Arm and Side Squeeze

1. Squeeze your left arm against your side (the side of your chest). Imagine you are holding a sponge in your armpit. Do this *now*.
2. *Let go.*
3. Pause--attend to the sensations that go with relaxation.
4. Begin your slow, soothing muscle talk.
5. Repeat the cycle.

Right Arm Squeeze

1. While keeping the rest of your body relaxed, bend your right arm at the elbow, touching your shoulder with your hand. Tense up the lower and upper right arm, *now*.
2. *Let go.*
3. Pause--there is nothing for you to do but let your muscles become more and more relaxed.
4. Begin your slow, soothing muscle talk.
5. Repeat the cycle.

Left Arm Squeeze

1. While keeping the rest of your body relaxed, bend your left arm at the elbow, touching your shoulder with your hand. Tense up the lower and upper left arm, *now*.
2. *Let go.*
3. Pause--quietly attend.
4. Begin your slow, soothing muscle talk.
5. Repeat the cycle.

Right Hand Squeeze

1. While keeping the rest of your body relaxed, make a tight fist with your right hand. Do this *now*.
2. *Let go.*
3. Pause--enjoy the feelings you have created.
4. Begin your slow, soothing muscle talk.
5. Repeat the cycle.

Left Hand Squeeze

1. While keeping the rest of your body relaxed, make a tight fist with your left hand. Do this *now*.
2. *Let go.*
3. Pause--let the tension begin to flow.
4. Begin your slow, soothing muscle talk.
5. Repeat the cycle.

Right Leg Squeeze

1. Direct your attention to your right leg. While keeping the rest of your body relaxed, tighten it up. You might want to pull your right leg up against your chair. Or push it down (don't stretch it out). Do this *now*.
2. *Let go.*
3. Pause--quietly compare the difference between tension and relaxation.
4. Begin your slow, soothing muscle talk.
5. Repeat.

Left Leg Squeeze

1. Direct your attention to your left leg. While keeping the rest of your body relaxed, tighten it up. You might want to pull your right leg up against your chair. Or push it down (don't stretch it out). Do this *now*.
2. *Let go.*
3. Pause--quietly attend.
4. Begin your slow, soothing muscle talk.
5. Repeat.

Right Foot Squeeze

1. Tighten up your right foot and toes. Curl your toes and push down, *now*.
2. *Let go.*
3. There is nothing to do but let your muscles become more and more relaxed.
4. Begin your slow, soothing muscle talk.
5. Repeat.

Left Foot Squeeze

1. Tighten up your left foot and toes. Curl your toes and push down, *now*.
2. *Let go.*
3. Sink deeper and deeper into relaxation.
4. Begin your slow, soothing muscle talk.
5. Repeat.

Ending

Sit quietly for a few minutes. Then slowly open your eyes, stretch, and take a deep breath. This completes your relaxation sequence.

Lesson 3

Yogaform Stretching

Our second approach to relaxation is also very popular. Yoga, in one form or another, is the most widely used approach to relaxation in the East. However, traditional yoga is more than an approach to relaxation. It is a complex mixture of religion, psychology, philosophy, dietary practices, sexual practices, as well as a variety of stretching exercises. Yogaform stretching is much simpler. The only objective is to slowly, smoothly, and gently stretch and unstretch major muscle groups. In contrast to isometric squeeze relaxation, which relies on a "tense-let go" rebound to produce relaxation, yogaform stretching actually stretches out muscle tension. It's as if each tense muscle group were a tightly coiled spring. You loosen it by gently pulling, stretching, and unstretching.

We will stretch the very same muscles we squeezed in the previous lesson. This is so you can more easily compare and contrast the effects of these exercises (and remember which muscle groups to work on). For each muscle group, we will use these three steps:

1. Slowly, smoothly, and gently stretch one muscle group, keeping the rest of the body relaxed. Create a nice good stretch. Then hold the stretch for about five seconds. Then, very slowly, smoothly, and gently let go of your stretch. Take your time. Your unstretching movement should take about as long as your stretching--about 15 to 25 seconds.
2. When finished, rest for about 10 seconds, quietly repeating whatever relaxation phrases you desire.
3. Repeat on the same muscle group before continuing.

Once again, here are some relaxation words you might consider for your soothing muscle talk. Select your phrases after you have had a little experience with yogaform stretching. Most people select a different set of relaxation phrases for different exercises.

Some Relaxing Words

Absorbed	Composed	Floating	Letting go	Restored
At ease	Concentrated	Flowing	Loose	Safe
Aware	Conscious	Focused	Meditative	Serene
Balanced	Contented	Free	Mellow	Smooth
Calm	Deep	Gentle	Peaceful	Soothed
Carefree	Dreamy	Healthy	Pleasant	Tingling
Centered	Drowsy	In control	Quiet	Tranquil
Cleansed	Easy	In harmony	Refreshed	Unhurried
Clear	Far away	Invigorated	Relaxed	Unworried
Comfortable	Flexible	Laid back	Rested	Warm

Here is your entire script for yogaform stretching.

Yogaform Stretching Script

Shoulder Stretch

1. First attend to your shoulders. While keeping the rest of your body relaxed, raise your arms in front of you, as if you were about to hug a large pillow to your chest. Slowly, smoothly, and gently, raise and cross your arms. Hug more and more tightly so you can feel a nice stretch along your shoulders and upper back. Then, slowly, smoothly, and gently unstretch.
2. Now quietly rest and enjoy the feelings you have created. Begin your slow, soothing muscle talk.
3. Repeat the cycle.

Back of Neck Stretch

1. Attend to the muscles in the back of your neck. Slowly, smoothly, and gently stretch them by gently tilting your head forward. Feel the muscles in the back of your neck stretch. Do not force your head down, simply let gravity pull the heavy weight. There is nothing you have to do but attend to the stretching sensations. Then, slowly, smoothly, and gently release the stretch. Return your head to an upright position.

2. Begin your slow, soothing muscle talk.
3. Repeat the cycle.

Face Stretch

1. Attend to the muscles in your face. Make an ugly face by slowly, smoothly, and gently opening your entire face. Very gently, open your jaws, mouth, and eyebrows while sticking your tongue out. Stretch more and more. And slowly, smoothly, and gently release your stretch.
2. Begin your slow, soothing muscle talk.
3. Repeat the cycle.

Front of Neck Stretch

1. Attend to the muscles of the front of your neck. While keeping the rest of your body relaxed, let your head gently begin to fall back. Do not force it back, simply let gravity do the work for you, pulling further and further. Notice the gentle stretch you can create in the front of your neck. And then release your stretch. Slowly, smoothly, and gently, return your head to an upright position.
2. Begin your slow, soothing muscle talk.
3. Repeat the cycle.

Back Stretch

1. Let both arms hang limply by your sides. Slowly, smoothly, and gently bow over in front of you. Do not force yourself down. Simply let gravity pull your torso down, more and more. Feel your back stretch as your head and torso sink lower. Then slowly, smoothly, and gently return to an upright position.
2. Begin your slow, soothing muscle talk.
3. Repeat the cycle.

Stomach and Chest Stretch

1. This time stretch your stomach and chest by extending them out in front of you. Arch your back and stick your stomach and chest out further and further. Slowly, smoothly, and gently, create a nice, complete stretch. And then gently return your stretch.

2. Begin your slow, soothing muscle talk.
3. Repeat the cycle.

Right Arm and Side Stretch

1. Let both arms hang limply by your side. Slowly, smoothly, and gently raise your left arm, like the hand of a clock, or the wing of a bird, further and further. Let your left arm raise into the air until it is reaching and pointing to the sky. And then reach and point, creating a good complete stretch all along your arm and side. When you are finished, gently return your arm. Slowly, smoothly, and gently return to the original resting position.
2. Begin your slow, soothing muscle talk.
3. Repeat the cycle.

Left Arm and Side Stretch

1. This time, stretch and unstretch your left arm and side, just as you stretched and unstretched your right arm and side.
2. Begin your slow, soothing muscle talk.
3. Repeat the cycle.

Right Arm Stretch

1. Rest both arms in your lap. Focus on your right arm. Slowly, smoothly, and gently slide your right hand down your leg toward your knee. Gently reach your right arm in front of you. Reach and stretch, further and further. Then, slowly, smoothly, and gently unstretch, returning your arm to your resting position.
2. Begin your slow, soothing muscle talk.
3. Repeat the cycle.

Left Arm Stretch

1. Slowly, smoothly, and gently slide your left hand down your leg toward your knee. Gently reach your left arm in front of you. Reach and stretch, further and further. Then, slowly, smoothly, and gently unstretch, returning your arm to your resting position.
2. Begin your slow, soothing muscle talk.
3. Repeat the cycle.

Right Hand Stretch

1. Rest both hands in your lap. Slowly, smoothly, and gently open your right hand and fingers. Stretch completely, and then gently unstretch.
2. Begin your slow, soothing muscle talk.
3. Repeat the cycle.

Left Hand Stretch

1. Slowly, smoothly, and gently open your left hand and fingers. Stretch completely, and then gently unstretch.
2. Begin your slow, soothing muscle talk.
3. Repeat the cycle.

Right Leg Stretch

1. Direct your attention to your right leg. Slowly, smoothly, and gently stretch your right leg in front of you. Stretch further and further. Then, slowly, smoothly, and gently unstretch.
2. Begin your slow, soothing muscle talk.
3. Repeat the cycle.

Left Leg Stretch

1. Slowly, smoothly, and gently stretch your left leg in front of you. Stretch further and further. Then, slowly, smoothly, and gently unstretch.
2. Begin your slow, soothing muscle talk.
3. Repeat the cycle.

Right Foot Stretch

1. Rest both feet flat on the floor. Focus on the right foot and while keeping the heel on the floor, slowly, smoothly, and gently raise your toes as if strings were pulling them up. Pull higher and higher. Then slowly, smoothly, and gently unstretch.
2. Begin your slow, soothing muscle talk.
3. Repeat the cycle.

Left Foot Stretch

1. Focus on the left foot and while keeping the heel on the floor, slowly, smoothly, and gently raise your toes as if strings were pulling them up. Pull higher and higher. Then slowly, smoothly, and gently unstretch.
2. Begin your slow, soothing muscle talk.
3. Repeat the cycle.

Ending

You are now finished with the complete yogaform stretching sequence. Take a few minutes to enjoy the pleasant feelings of relaxation you have created. Then slowly open your eyes.

Lesson 4

Breathing Exercises

Most forms of relaxation, both traditional and contemporary, incorporate breathing exercises. The reason is simple. When we are under stress, we tend to breathe more through the chest. In contrast, relaxed breathing makes greater use of the diaphragm, a drum-like muscle that separates the lungs from the stomach. When you breathe with your diaphragm, it may seem as if you are breathing in and out through your abdomen, filling and emptying it of air. In fact, as the diaphragm pushes down, in piston-like fashion, it not only draws air into the lungs, but gently pushes the abdomen below.

Relaxed breathing also has a special pattern. When we are tense, the pace of breathing may be too rapid or too slow. Pauses may be too short or too long. We may breathe too slowly or too rapidly. And often breathing is uneven, rather than rhythmical.

Breathing exercises are designed to teach us to make greater use of the diaphragm, breathe more evenly, and at a more relaxing pattern. We will explore four exercises: bowing and breathing, breathing with gentle sniffs, breathing out through the lips, and deep breathing. Each exercise will follow these steps:

1. Slowly, smoothly, and gently breathe in the way described. Spend about two or three minutes with each exercise.
2. When finished, rest for about 10 seconds, quietly repeating whatever relaxation phrases you desire.

Once again, here is your list of relaxation words. You may use them in your relaxation self-talk.

Some Relaxing Words

Absorbed	Composed	Floating	Letting go	Restored
At ease	Concentrated	Flowing	Loose	Safe
Aware	Conscious	Focused	Meditative	Serene
Balanced	Contented	Free	Mellow	Smooth
Calm	Deep	Gentle	Peaceful	Soothed
Carefree	Dreamy	Healthy	Pleasant	Tingling
Centered	Drowsy	In control	Quiet	Tranquil
Cleansed	Easy	In harmony	Refreshed	Unhurried
Clear	Far away	Invigorated	Relaxed	Unworried
Comfortable	Flexible	Laid back	Rested	Warm

Breathing Exercises Script

Bowing and Breathing

1. Sit up straight in a relaxed position. Let both arms hang in a limp and relaxed position to each side. Take a good deep breath. Then slowly, smoothly, and gently bow forward. Do not force yourself; let gravity pull your body down toward your knees. As you bow, gently let the air out, very smoothly and slowly. When you are ready, slowly, smoothly, and gently sit up, while taking in a good breath of air.
2. Begin relaxing self-talk.
3. Repeat.

Breathing with Gentle Sniffs

1. Let your breathing become more and more smooth and relaxed. As you inhale, breathe in with short, gentle sniffs, almost as if you were breathing a delicate flower. After taking a full breath, gently breathe out. Continue breathing this way for about one minute.
2. Begin relaxing self-talk.
3. Repeat.

Breathing out through the Lips

1. Let your breathing become more and more easy and relaxed. Slowly take in a deep breath. As you exhale, gently open your lips very slightly, and breathe out through your lips. Imagine you are blowing on a candle flame, just enough to

make the flame flicker and not go out.   After you have exhaled, inhale once again through your nose.   Continue breathing this way for about one minute.

2.   Begin relaxing self-talk.

3.   Repeat.

Deep Breathing

1.   Slowly, smoothly, and gently take in a full deep breath.   Take your time.   There is no need to hurry.   Pause.   And then gently let go, gently letting all of the air out.   Notice the smooth flow of air moving in past your nostrils, and into and out of your lungs.   Pause.   When you are ready, breathe in again.   Continue breathing this way, fully, evenly, and slowly, for about a minute.

2.   Begin relaxing self-talk.

3.   Repeat.

Ending

You are now finished with the complete breathing sequence.   Take a few minutes to enjoy the pleasant feelings of relaxation you have created.   Then slowly open your eyes.

Thematic Imagery Exercises

Imagery can be a particularly rewarding and interesting approach to relaxation. It is also an approach most people know something about. Have you ever simply sat back and let your mind wander in a peaceful daydream? That is imagery. Specifically, you select a relaxing theme, and then dwell with it. However, there are some specific rules for imagery. Make sure the theme is passive, simple, and relaxing (sitting on a beach rather than playing baseball). And involve all of your senses--what you see, hear, feel against your skin, and smell.

There are four general imagery themes you might want to consider: travel imagery, outdoor/nature imagery, water imagery, and indoor imagery. Below are specific examples of each:

Travel Imagery
   Relaxing on a train
   Relaxing on an airplane
   Your private limousine
   Relaxing on a hot air balloon
   On a cloud or floating through air
   Your favorite vacation spot
   A trip through outer space (to the moon, fantasy planet)
   Underwater in a submarine

Nature/Outdoor Imagery
   Sitting on a grassy plain
   The farm
   Relaxing in the woods
   The garden

The nature trail
The campfire
Watching the night sky on a hill
On top of a hill/mountain overlooking a valley
Looking at the moon

Water Imagery
Resting on a beach by the ocean
Lying on a boat far out at sea
Fishing by the river
On the banks of a stream
Beside a small pond
A relaxing pool or tub
In a mist or fog.
Walking in the rain

Indoor Imagery
The bed/sofa/chair
Resting by the fireplace in a warm winter cabin
A restful room in the vacation house of your dreams
A church, temple, or cathedral
The porch/balcony
High in a skyscraper
The treehouse
Your childhood home

Once you select your theme, introduce details involving the senses. For example, if your theme is *On the Banks of a River*, you might include the following details:

What you see
The water rushing down the stream
An occasional fish
The blue sky and large, soft clouds
Green trees by the bank
Birds in the sky

What you hear
The rushing water
A breeze flowing through the trees
A bird singing

What you feel touching your skin
   The warm sun
   The cool breeze
   The spray of the water
   The soft grass

What you smell
   The clean scent of water
   Pine trees
   Flowers

On a separate piece of paper, list the details of your imagery theme. Remember to include all of the senses.

When you practice your imagery, simply close your eyes and involve all of your senses. From time to time let a special relaxation phrase float through your mind. Do not be concerned if none come to you while you are practicing. Simply repeat a few phrases before and after your imagery session. Here, once again are some words you might want to consider for your relaxation phrases.

Some Relaxing Words

Absorbed	Composed	Floating	Letting go	Restored
At ease	Concentrated	Flowing	Loose	Safe
Aware	Conscious	Focused	Meditative	Serene
Balanced	Contented	Free	Mellow	Smooth
Calm	Deep	Gentle	Peaceful	Soothed
Carefree	Dreamy	Healthy	Pleasant	Tingling
Centered	Drowsy	In control	Quiet	Tranquil
Cleansed	Easy	In harmony	Refreshed	Unhurried
Clear	Far away	Invigorated	Relaxed	Unworried
Comfortable	Flexible	Laid back	Rested	Warm

Ending

You are now finished with the complete imagery sequence. Take a few minutes to enjoy the pleasant feelings of relaxation you have created. Then slowly open your eyes.

Lesson 6

Meditation Exercises

Meditation is perhaps the simplest relaxation exercise to describe. It is also one of the most difficult to practice. When most people try to meditate, their first mistake is to attempt to do too much. In fact, to meditate all you have to do is this:

Calmly attend to a simple stimulus
Gently return your attention after every distraction
Again and again and again

You may have already meditated without even knowing it. For example, here is a very meditative experience:

I am outdoors admiring the sunset. I have put my cares and concerns aside. I have no urge to think about or figure out the sunset. I simply attend, calmly and peacefully attend.

Meditation begins with a simple stimulus, a sunset for example. Any stimulus would work, as long as it is sufficiently simple so not to stir up associations. For this reason, it is not a good idea to meditate on the imagery themes suggested in the previous lesson. Thematic imagery is rich and complex, whereas meditation is very simple. We will introduce five meditation stimuli: rocking, breathing, a relaxing word, a visual image, and an external stimulus.

Perhaps the most common experience among those who practice meditation is distraction. Your mind will wander. You will start thinking about something other than your stimulus. You will notice outside noises. It is OK to be distracted while meditating. Meditation is not a concentration exercise. The goal is not to glue your attention on your stimulus as if you were playing a video game. Let yourself be distracted. And after every distraction calmly return your attention to your stimulus. Meditation is not so much a concentration exercise as it is an exercise in returning attention after every distraction, an exercise in coming home.

When you meditate you might want to think of what happens when you take a small child for a walk on a path through the woods. The child may innocently wander from the path, again and again. Each time the child wanders, you gently and lovingly return him without making a big thing of it. You realize that eventually the child will learn to stay on the path, and that each wandering gives you a chance to reinforce the returning motion again. Similarly, each time you return your attention to your meditative stimulus, you gently condition your mind to attend for longer periods of time. Once again, it is OK to be distracted. It is only through being distracted that you have the opportunity to practice returning attention, and build your meditative skills.

This week we will try a different meditation every day. Simply meditate for 15-20 minutes after reading the instructions. Since meditation is a very passive exercise, quietly repeating relaxing words and phrases would be distracting. For this reason, relaxing self-talk instructions have been omitted.

BASIC MEDITATIONS

Rocking Meditation

Think of all of the times in life you have found the motion of *gently rocking* meditative. For example, you might recall peacefully resting in a rocking chair, or quietly floating in a boat on a lake. Or think of a small child, gently rocking in a mother's arms. In this meditation all you have to do is gently rock back and forth, and easily attend to your rocking. As you continue, let your rocking gradually grow more and more gentle until you are barely rocking at all. Let your rocking become even more gentle until someone looking at you would not even know you are rocking. This meditation is very easy. Gently attend to your rocking motion, and after every distraction gently return your attention . . . again and again and again.

Breathing Meditation

Let your breathing become more and more gentle. There is no reason to force yourself to breathe in any particular way. Simply breathe in a full and relaxed manner. Every time you exhale, calmly let the word "one" easily float through your mind. Do not force the word to repeat in any particular way. Simply let the word float by in its own way, at its own volume and speed. All you have to do is gently attend, almost as if you were attending to an echo. Once again this exercise can be summarized: "exhale . . . o-n-e . . . inhale . . . exhale . . . o-n-e . . . inhale . . . exhale . . . o-n-e . . ."

Meditating on a Relaxing Word

In this meditation begin by selecting a simple relaxing word. For example, the words "calm" or "peace" would do just fine. When meditating, let this word simply float through your mind, like an echo. Let it go at its own speed and volume. All you have to do is attend, and return your attention every time your mind wanders.

Meditation on a Visual Image

Begin by selecting a simple, unchanging mental image. For example, you might want to think of a candle flame, a pond, a star in the night sky, or even a religious symbol. Avoid complex images such as those employed in thematic imagery. Calmly attend to your image, returning your attention after every distraction.

Meditation on an External Stimulus

Slowly open your eyes halfway. Easily gaze on a simple external object. Whenever your mind wanders, gently return.

Ending

You are now finished with the meditation sequence. Take a few minutes to enjoy the pleasant feelings of relaxation you have created. Then slowly open your eyes.

Developing a
Relaxation Sequence

Now is the time for you to construct a relaxation program tailored to your needs. We begin by selecting which of the exercises you have tried that seem to work best for you. Below is a list of all of the exercises in this program. Which would you like to use?

Isometric Squeeze Exercises

> Shoulder Squeeze
> Back of Neck Squeeze
> Face Squeeze
> Front of Neck Squeeze
> Back Squeeze
> Stomach and Chest Squeeze
> Arm and Side Squeeze
> Arm Squeeze
> Hand Squeeze
> Leg Squeeze
> Foot Squeeze

Yogaform Stretching Exercises

> Shoulder Stretch
> Back of Neck Stretch
> Face Stretch
> Front of Neck Stretch
> Back Stretch
> Stomach and Chest Stretch

Arm and Side Stretch
Arm Stretch
Hand Stretch
Leg Stretch
Foot Stretch

Breathing Exercises

Bowing and Breathing
Breathing with Gentle Sniffs
Breathing Out through the Lips
Deep Breathing

Thematic Imagery

Meditation

Rocking Meditation
Breathing Meditation
Meditation on a Relaxing Word
Meditation on a Visual Image
Meditation on an External Stimulus

Now take another look at the exercises you have selected. You will need no fewer than five and no more than ten exercises. Go back to your selected exercises and pick a final assortment of five. Finally, take a look at what you have chosen. In what order should you practice your exercises? Although many sequences are possible, it is generally a good idea to start with the most active and end with relatively passive exercises.

Lesson 8

Mini-relaxation

Once you have practiced your complete relaxation sequence for at least a week, you are ready to construct a five-minute mini-relaxation sequence to practice outside of your regularly scheduled practice time. Think of your mini-relaxation as an abbreviated version of your complete relaxation program. Include in it no more than five key exercises from your complete program in any order you feel is best. For example, a complete program might include the following exercises:

Back of Neck Squeeze
Face Squeeze
Front of Neck Squeeze
Shoulder Squeeze
Shoulder Stretch
Arm and Side Stretch
Deep Breathing
Breathing Out through the Lips
Imagery: *Travel in a Balloon*

A mini-relaxation might include the following abbreviated sequence:

Back of Neck Squeeze
Shoulder Squeeze
Breathing Out through the Lips
Imagery: *Travel in a Balloon*

Notice how this sequence abbreviates the main components of the complete sequence. It contains key squeezing, stretching, and breathing exercises as well as imagery.

Practice your mini-relaxation throughout the day at strategic times. For example, while waiting for the bus, during your coffee break, before lunch, and so on.

Lesson 9

The Relaxation Philosophy

A relaxation philosophy consists of enduring beliefs, values, and commitments conducive to deep and generalized relaxation. Affirmations of such a philosophy can be effectively woven into your relaxation sequence as an introduction or conclusion. Quietly repeating affirmations of your philosophy can even be used in place of a mini-relaxation.

First it is important to consider what beliefs, values, and commitments you might have that are not conducive to relaxation. Here are some my students have shared over the years:

"I must be in control at all times." (How can you let go and relax if you feel like you must be in control?)

"Relaxation must have an immediate payoff for me." (Relaxation takes time and practice to work.)

"When I get distracted during relaxation, this means that it isn't working." (Getting distracted is OK during a relaxation exercise. Simply return to the exercise.)

"The most effective route to health and success is to strive to be perfect in all things." (Nobody can be perfect at everything. Striving for perfection can create needless tension not conducive to relaxation.)

"I am not capable of making my life better." (With practice, nearly everyone can learn to relax. Giving up obviously is not a way to master a skill.)

"Things will automatically get better on their own." (There is nothing magical about relaxation. Once again, movement and growth come through practice).

Here are affirmations of personal relaxation philosophies:

"My selfish worries are distractions that fog awareness of a deeper reality."

"God loves me and has a plan for my life."

"The meaning of life becomes more apparent to me in the quiet of relaxation."

"My urgent concerns seem less important when seen in broader perspective."

"There are more important things than my everyday hassles."

"At the deepest level I can feel at peace with myself; I am an OK person."

"I choose to live one day at a time and not worry about things that cannot be changed."

"I choose to quit creating unnecessary pain and tension for myself by ignoring my true feelings.

"God's will be done."

It is easy to develop a mini-relaxation based on your relaxation philosophy. Begin with one relaxation exercise selected from your complete sequence. Follow this with three or four relaxing phrases. End with a simple (one-sentence) affirmation of your relaxation philosophy. Simply let your affirmation float easily through your mind, as if it were a meditation word. Here are some examples of mini-relaxation affirmations.

Example: I begin with three or four minutes of deep relaxation. I then quietly repeat the following phrases to myself:

"Sink more and more deeply into relaxation."

"Let go of feelings of tightness and tension."

"Become more and more open to the possibilities within."

"It feels good to relax."

I then conclude by gently affirming my relaxation philosophy:

"Live one day at a time. Do not worry about things that can't be changed."

Example: I introduce my mini-relaxation with a good shoulder squeeze. I tense up, and then let go of needless tension. After repeating this a few times, I think these phrases to myself:

"Attend more and more to the feelings of relaxation you have created."

"It is good to let go of needless tension."
"Trust the feelings of relaxation within."
"It is OK to let go and become more and more relaxed."

I end with a simple prayer that affirms my relaxation philosophy:

"Quietly put your troubles in God's hands and let God's will be done."

Part 4

Exercises

Exercises for Chapter 1

INDIVIDUAL EXERCISE 1.1:
THE STRESS TEST

In order to develop our stress management skills, and determine when techniques are working, we will need to frequently measure our level of stress by taking the Stress TEST (Short for Stress Thought, Emotions, and Symptoms Test). Here it is.

The items on the following page describe experiences people often have. Please read each carefully and indicate the extent to which it fits how you *typically* or *generally* feel. Rate all the items by putting numbers in the blanks to the left. Use the following "10-point scale."

HOW WELL DOES THE ITEM YOU ARE READING
FIT HOW YOU TYPICALLY OR GENERALLY FEEL?

0 = NOT AT ALL
1 = In between
2 = In between
3 = In between
4 = In between
5 = MODERATELY
6 = In between
7 = In between
8 = In between
9 = In between
10 = EXTREMELY WELL

Thought and Worry

___ 1. I worry too much about things that don't really matter.
___ 2. I have difficulty keeping troublesome thoughts out of my mind.
___ 3. Anxiety-provoking thoughts run through my mind.
___ 4. Unimportant thoughts run through my mind and bother me.
___ 5. I worry about things even when I know worrying isn't making them better.
___ 6. I find it difficult to control negative thoughts.

Negative Emotion

___ 7. I feel distressed (discouraged, downhearted, or sad).
___ 8. I feel irritated or angry (annoyed, provoked, mad, or defiant).
___ 9. I feel contempt.
___ 10. I feel distaste or disgust.
___ 11. I feel shy or sheepish.
___ 12. I feel fearful.
___ 13. I feel depressed.
___ 14. I feel anxious.

Physical Symptoms

___ 15. My heart beats fast, hard, or irregularly.
___ 16. My breathing feels hurried, shallow, or uneven.
___ 17. My muscles feel tight, tense, or clenched up (furrowed brow, making fist, clenching jaws, etc.).
___ 18. I feel restless and fidgety (tapping fingers or feet, fingering things, pacing, shifting in seat, chewing or biting, blinking).
___ 19. I feel tense or self-conscious when I say or do something.
___ 20. I perspire too much or feel too warm.
___ 21. I feel the need to go to the rest room even when I don't have to.
___ 22. I feel uncoordinated.
___ 23. My mouth feels dry.
___ 24. I feel tired, fatigued, worn out, or exhausted.
___ 25. I have a headache.
___ 26. I feel unfit or heavy.
___ 27. My back aches.
___ 28. My shoulders, neck, or back feels tense.
___ 29. The condition of my skin seems worse (too oily, blemishes).
___ 30. My eyes are watering or teary.
___ 31. My stomach is nervous and uncomfortable.
___ 32. I have lost my appetite.

Your Scores

Now, add your scores for each of the three sections on the Stress TEST. Thought and Worry: ___ Negative Emotion: ___ Physical Symptoms: ___ Here is where you fit compared with others.

Men

Thought Score	Emotion Score	Symptom Score	Level	
55	60	145	10	HI
45	47	95	9	
36	40	76	8	
31	35	66	7	
28	31	55	6	
23	25	45	5	
19	21	36	4	
15	16	26	3	
11	11	19	2	
8	5	8	1	
2	2	3	0	LO

Women

Thought Score	Emotion Score	Symptom Score	Level	
57	63	154	10	HI
49	51	101	9	
42	39	83	8	
35	32	69	7	
30	27	56	6	
27	22	48	5	
23	18	40	4	
17	14	31	3	
13	10	19	2	
7	6	9	1	
2	3	4	0	LO

NOTE: Percentiles are in the right column. Norm sample consisted of 224 males and 290 females (age means = 21.87 and 23.38; *SDs* = 9.46 and 8.99). For those over 35, scores will tend to be overestimated. Subjects were students at Chicago's Roosevelt University and Harper College in Palatine, IL. We wish to extend our thanks to Michael Ostrowski, PhD for his considerable help in collecting data.

The column on the far right is labeled "level." This shows how high or low your score is compared with others. For example, a woman with a stress thought score of 27 would have a stress level of 5, which is average. This can also be expressed on a simple scale:

Stressful
Thinking Level

|-|-|-|-|-|-|-|-|-|-|
0 1 2 3 4 5 6 7 8 9 10

On the charts below indicate your overall levels of stressful thinking, negative emotion, and physical symptoms:

Stressful	Stressful	Stressful
Thinking Level	Emotion Level	Symptom Level
|-|-|-|-|-|-|-|-|-|-|	|-|-|-|-|-|-|-|-|-|-|	|-|-|-|-|-|-|-|-|-|-|
0 1 2 3 4 5 6 7 8 9 10	0 1 2 3 4 5 6 7 8 9 10	0 1 2 3 4 5 6 7 8 9 10

What do your scores mean? The scales provide a rough comparison with others. However, your score should not be seen as a final "diagnosis"--no single paper and pencil test can do that. A high score can be caused by many things other than stress. Perhaps you have had a bad day. Maybe you are more willing than most to share your feelings on a questionnaire, resulting in a score that appears high. If you are concerned about your stress score, it might be a good idea to see a qualified mental health professional. He or she can help you determine if stress is a problem, and what you can do about it.

What if your score is especially low? Once again, it is unwise to view this test as a final diagnosis. Many people experience relatively low levels of stress. Others are under stress, but are simply unaware of it; for them stress is a "silent problem," one that may well emerge later on. Once again, if you are confused or concerned about your stress score, it can be a good idea to see a qualified mental health professional.

Stress Scales

The Stress TEST provides a measure of overall stress, how you generally feel most of the time . It can be useful to obtain a measure of how you feel at any one moment. From time to time this workbook will ask you to take a quick "snapshot" of your stress level on a ten-point scale. For example, at the present moment, what is your overall level of stress Thought? Where would you place yourself on the following scale?

Stressful
Thinking Level
|-|-|-|-|-|-|-|-|-|-|-|
0 1 2 3 4 5 6 7 8 9 10

Now rate your present level of negative emotion on the following scale.

Stressful
Emotion Level
|-|-|-|-|-|-|-|-|-|-|-|
0 1 2 3 4 5 6 7 8 9 10

And rate your level of physical symptoms.

Stressful
Symptom Level
|-|-|-|-|-|-|-|-|-|-|-|
0 1 2 3 4 5 6 7 8 9 10

These ten-point scales are much quicker than the complete 32-item stress TEST we just tried. However, try to think of each scale as measuring what the complete test measures, only in summary form. That is, if you scored high on the stress TEST physical symptoms scale, perhaps higher than 90 percent of those taking this test, you might make your quick physical symptom rating a 9. Similarly, a TEST level at the 50 percent level might correspond to a score of 5, and so on. Quick 10-point ratings will be useful for rating the degree of stressfulness of specific situations as well as the overall effects of various stress management and relaxation exercises to be presented later.

INDIVIDUAL EXERCISE 1.2:
THINKING ABOUT STRESS REACTIONS

Different people experience different stress TEST reactions. And there are some reactions most people share. In this exercise, see how you would answer the following questions:

What are your stress reactions?
What reactions might serve as useful early warning signals?
Are any reactions less useful as early warning signals? Why?
What stress reactions are most common among people you know?

INDIVIDUAL EXERCISE 1.3:
CAUSAL LINKS AMONG STRESS TEST REACTIONS

Stress reactions are often interrelated. Have you ever found that worry (a Thought reaction) can contribute to tension in the back and shoulders (a Symptom reaction)? Or has a physical symptom, such as a continued stomach ache, ever contributed to worry? Similarly, can you think of times where an emotion (perhaps anxiety) has led to a symptom (a headache), or times where symptoms have contributed to anxiety?

INDIVIDUAL EXERCISE 1.4:
COSTS OF STRESS

As shown in Chapter 1, stress can have many costs. Excess stress can contribute to illness, which results in lost work time, increased medical and insurance bills, and so on. Stress can reduce efficiency and increase accident-proneness at work. Alcohol and drug abuse can be seen as maladaptive ways of attempting to reduce stress. What costs of stress can you identify?

OPTIONAL RELAXATION ASSIGNMENT:
PREPARING FOR RELAXATION TRAINING

In order to obtain maximum benefit from this book, it is important that you master a form of relaxation that fits your needs. If you are working with a therapist or trainer, follow the relaxation program they present. An alternative is to complete the relaxation program offered in Part 3 of this book. Or you may wish to acquire and use the book, *Relaxation Dynamics* (Smith, 1989).

If you are following the relaxation instructions presented in Part 3 of this book, read Lesson 1. If you are completing *Relaxation Dynamics*, read Lessons 1-6.

Exercises for Chapter 2

INDIVIDUAL EXERCISE 2.1:
THE STRESS SCRIPT

On the following page is a blank stress script. In this exercise write a script describing what actually happened (problems and all) in a recent stress situation. (Fill out as much as applies.)

GENERAL SITUATION:

OTHER PERSON

    BEHAVIOR LINE:
    SPEECH LINE:

YOU

OTHER PERSON

    BEHAVIOR LINE:
    SPEECH LINE:

YOU

    BEHAVIOR LINE:
    SPEECH LINE:
    FEELING LINE:
    THOUGHT LINE:

INDIVIDUAL EXERCISE 2.2:
THE STRESS SCRIPT DIARY

At the end of each day for the next week describe a stressful encounter you had involving another person. Here it will not be necessary to write a complete script. A capsule summary of important highlights can do. Provide important Behavior, Speech, Feeling, and Thought Lines, indicating which is which in the blanks provided. Then, give yourself an overall Stress TEST rating for the situation. The last task is to give yourself an overall Stress TEST rating for the whole day, that is, you generally felt most of the day.

The goal of this exercise is *not* to think of examples of good stress management or coping. Report everything, the good, bad, and the ugly. However, make sure your reports follow the rules of good script writing. That is, your BEHAVIOR LINES should describe behaviors (and not thoughts), your THOUGHT LINES should describe thoughts (and not behaviors), and so on.

To give you some practice, here are several capsule scripts, both good and poorly written so you can see what mistakes to avoid.

EXAMPLE 1: Poorly Written Script

GENERAL SITUATION: Dealing with the garage mechanic

OTHER PERSON:

BEHAVIOR LINE: Storms out of office and verbally attacks me. Puts his stinking cigar in his mouth.
SPEECH LINE: Treats me very impolitely. He's acting like a complete idiot.

YOU

BEHAVIOR LINE: I keep my cool.
SPEECH LINE: I tell him what I think the problem is, and try to come to a solution.
FEELING LINE: I feel OK.
THOUGHT LINE: I try not to show I'm upset.

Analysis: This script violates a number of SCRIPT rules (Chapter 2):

> ___ *Simple*
> *NO Concrete*
> *NO Realistic*
> *NO Important*
> ___ *Personal*
> ___ *Timely*

First, concrete behaviors and speech are not described, just vague generalities. Second, the depiction "acting like a complete idiot" is surely an unrealistic exaggeration. And the detail concerning the cigar, although not particularly pleasant, is just not that important. Now look at this improved version:

EXAMPLE 1: Better Script

GENERAL SITUATION: Contesting a bill with the auto mechanic

OTHER PERSON: Mechanic

BEHAVIOR LINE: Hands me my bill and starts walking away.
SPEECH LINE: "Here you are sir. You can pay the cashier. Your car really had some problems."

YOU

BEHAVIOR LINE: I look the mechanic straight in the eye
SPEECH LINE: "Excuse me. I believe there is an error on this bill. I did not order a complete oil change."
FEELING LINE: I am getting anxious about this incident.
THOUGHT LINE: "He must think I won't study the bill."

EXAMPLE 2: Poorly Written Script

GENERAL SITUATION: Setting someone straight at work

OTHER PERSON: The person I share my office desk with

BEHAVIOR LINE: He acts cold and rude.
SPEECH LINE: Wants me to do his work.

YOU

BEHAVIOR LINE: To avoid doing his work for him
SPEECH LINE: I can't always do his work for him.
FEELING LINE: I get real upset.
THOUGHT LINE: Why does he always do this to me? I really can't stand this behavior. It really got bad last month.

Analysis: The Behavior Line, "To avoid doing his work for him" is not a behavior, but a general goal. Since goals often appear as thoughts (e.g., "I realize that I do not want to do his work for him"), they are Thought Lines. In addition, specific, concrete behaviors are not described. What does "act cold and rude" mean? Vague feelings ("real upset") are presented. The Speech Lines aren't Speech Lines at all; they do not specify what should be said. A bit of history ("It really got bad last month") is introduced. This script overstates the problem ("Why does he always do this to me?"). SCRIPT rating:

NO Simple
NO Concrete
NO Realistic
___ Important
___ Personal
___ Timely

EXAMPLE 2: Better Script

GENERAL SITUATION: Dealing with a coworker's request to do his work

OTHER PERSON

BEHAVIOR LINE: Coworker slams his desk drawer shut and throws his papers on desk.
SPEECH LINE: "I have a problem to deal with at home. I would like you to complete this project for me."

YOU

BEHAVIOR LINE: I frown, and look down.
SPEECH LINE: "OK, I'll be happy to do the work. Just leave it here."
FEELING LINE: My stomach is beginning to churn. I feel confused.
THOUGHT LINE: "I'm not going to let him get away with making me do his work. But I don't want him to think I'm selfish."

EXAMPLE 3 Poorly Written Script

GENERAL SITUATION: Trying to be more sociable

OTHER PERSON: Someone at a party

BEHAVIOR LINE: He looks approachable.
SPEECH LINE: He asks me the time.

YOU

BEHAVIOR LINE: I get myself ready to break the ice.
SPEECH LINE: "About midnight. Nice party, isn't it?"
FEELING LINE: Butterflies
THOUGHT LINE: Maybe he'll reject me.

Analysis: Well, this script is a little better. At least we know something about what is said. However, the other person's Speech Line should actually indicate the words said. In other words, Speech Lines should always by surrounded by quotation marks. And the Behavior Line "break the ice" is not concrete. What SCRIPT ratings would you give?

___ *Simple*
___ *Concrete*
___ *Realistic*
___ *Important*
___ *Personal*
___ *Timely*

EXAMPLE 3: Better Script

GENERAL SITUATION: Meeting someone at a party

OTHER PERSON: Interested other person

> BEHAVIOR LINE: Turns to me and asks me a question.
> SPEECH LINE: "Excuse me, could you tell me the time?"

YOU

> BEHAVIOR LINE: I turn and look directly at him.
> SPEECH LINE: "Yes, its about midnight. Are you with anyone tonight?"
> FEELING LINE: I feel queasy in my stomach, and very sheepish.
> THOUGHT LINE: "He looks attractive. I hope he doesn't reject me."

Stress Diary: DAY ___

[Note: This is a diary template. To use, make seven copies, one for each day of the week. Do not put your responses on this page]

GENERAL SITUATION:

OTHER PERSON (If Any):

> BEHAVIOR LINE:
> SPEECH LINE:

YOU

> BEHAVIOR LINE:
> SPEECH LINE:
> FEELING LINE:
> THOUGHT LINE:

Stress TEST levels

Rate your level of negative thought or worry:

During Situation	Overall Level for Day
|-|-|-|-|-|-|-|-|-|-|	|-|-|-|-|-|-|-|-|-|-|
0 1 2 3 4 5 6 7 8 9 10	0 1 2 3 4 5 6 7 8 9 10

Rate your level of negative emotion:

During Situation	Overall Level for Day
|-|-|-|-|-|-|-|-|-|-|	|-|-|-|-|-|-|-|-|-|-|
0 1 2 3 4 5 6 7 8 9 10	0 1 2 3 4 5 6 7 8 9 10

Rate your level of physical symptoms:

During Situation	Overall Level for Day
|-|-|-|-|-|-|-|-|-|-|	|-|-|-|-|-|-|-|-|-|-|
0 1 2 3 4 5 6 7 8 9 10	0 1 2 3 4 5 6 7 8 9 10

INDIVIDUAL EXERCISE 2.3:
BRAINSTORMING ALTERNATIVES

Stress-prone people often feel like they are in a rut, trapped, with no way out. One reason for this is they have not fully developed the skill of brainstorming alternatives. Their stress script might read: Encounter Problem Situation--Think of One Solution--Solution Doesn't Work--More Stress. In this exercise we will learn to add a line to this script: Brainstorm Alternatives. Here's how.

Brainstorming is a special way of problem solving that involves actively trying to think of a large number of possible solutions. However, to do this you must temporarily put aside critical thinking. Let yourself be creative. Think of *all* the alternatives you can, good, bad, and silly. Later you will pick which are best. Begin by taking one of the stress scripts from your diary. Describe it on the following page. Then comes the fun part. Brainstorm four alternative Thought, Speech, and Behavior Lines. Then go pack and circle those that seem most adaptive and realistic.

GENERAL SITUATION:

OTHER PERSON (IF ANY):

BEHAVIOR LINE:
SPEECH LINE:

YOU

   ORIGINAL BEHAVIOR LINE:
   ORIGINAL SPEECH LINE:
   ORIGINAL FEELING LINE:
   ORIGINAL THOUGHT LINE:

BRAINSTORMED ALTERNATIVES

   BEHAVIOR LINES:
      1.
      2.
      3.
      4.

   SPEECH LINES:
      1.
      2.
      3.
      4.

   THOUGHT LINES:
      1.
      2.
      3.
      4.

NOW, CIRCLE YOUR BEST ALTERNATIVE BEHAVIOR, SPEECH, AND THOUGHT LINES.

GROUP EXERCISE 2.4:
SCRIPT CONNECTIONS

Divide into teams of four. Each considers the following questions:

   What connections can you see in your experience of stress?
   How are Behavior, Thought, Feeling, and Speech Lines interconnected?
   Which script lines are most associated with which stress TEST patterns?

GROUP EXERCISE 2.5:
SCRIPT EVALUATIONS

Divide into teams of four. Each member shares a stress script. Other members discuss the script. Discussion topics include:

Does this script follow the rules described in the text? For example, do Behavior Lines include just behaviors, or also thoughts and feelings?

What are some of the payoffs of scripting a stress situation? How does this approach of thinking about stress differ from how people usually consider stress?

In the exercises so far, you have been asked to describe real-life scripts, both good and bad. Have any group members presented scripts that represent *good coping*? What approaches seem to work, and what approaches seem to be counterproductive?

What SCRIPT rules are followed?

OPTIONAL RELAXATION ASSIGNMENT:
ISOMETRIC SQUEEZE RELAXATION

If you are completing the relaxation program in Part 3 of this book, read Lesson 2. If you are completing the *Relaxation Dynamics* Program, do Lesson 7.

Exercises for Chapter 3

INDIVIDUAL EXERCISE 3.1:
THINKING OF EXAMPLES

Develop an assertive, nonassertive, and aggressive example for each of the 12 situations discussed in Chapter 3.

INDIVIDUAL EXERCISE 3.2:
STRESS/ASSERTIVENESS DIARY

Every day describe a stress situation that involved other people. Use the following Stress Diary format. First report what happened. If you were nonassertive or aggressive, rewrite your script so that it is more assertive.

Stress Diary: Example

GENERAL SITUATION: Protesting an overbilling

OTHER PERSON: Store Cashier

BEHAVIOR LINE: Hands me the bill
SPEECH LINE: "Do you wish to pay by check or credit card?"

YOU (what you actually did)

BEHAVIOR LINE: Look at bill. Turn away from cashier.
SPEECH LINE: "Uh, OK. I'll pay by check."
THOUGHT LINE: I'm being overcharged. Keep quiet. Don't

make a scene.
FEELING LINE: Anxiety

ASSERTIVENESS ANALYSIS

ASSERTIVE, NONASSERTIVE, OR AGGRESSIVE?:
Nonassertive
ROLE: Someone giving in, a child
GOAL: Not to make waves
NONVERBALS: Looking down and away. Soft, weak voice.

Stress TEST levels

Rate your level of negative thought or worry:

During Situation	Overall Level for Day
0 1 2 3 4 5 6 7 8 9 10	0 1 2 3 4 5 6 7 8 9 10

Rate your level of negative emotion:

During Situation	Overall Level for Day
0 1 2 3 4 5 6 7 8 9 10	0 1 2 3 4 5 6 7 8 9 10

Rate your level of physical symptoms:

During Situation	Overall Level for Day
0 1 2 3 4 5 6 7 8 9 10	0 1 2 3 4 5 6 7 8 9 10

YOU (rewritten assertively)

BEHAVIOR LINE: Face clerk directly. Look at her in the eyes.
SPEECH LINE: "Excuse me, but I would like you to add up this
bill again, and please check the price of this item."
FEELING LINE: Anxiety and determination
THOUGHT LINE: Even if wrong, I have the right to check this
bill.

ASSERTIVENESS ANALYSIS

PROBLEM-SOLVING GOAL: To get the bill corrected, if
wrong.
SELF-EXPRESSION GOAL: To make it clear I am questioning
the bill
NONVERBALS: Face and look directly at clerk

Stress Diary: DAY ___

[Make seven copies of this diary template, one for each day. Do not put your responses on this page.]

GENERAL SITUATION:

OTHER PERSON (IF ANY):

BEHAVIOR LINE:
SPEECH LINE:

YOU (what you actually did)

BEHAVIOR LINE:
SPEECH LINE:
FEELING LINE:
THOUGHT LINE:

ASSERTIVENESS ANALYSIS

ASSERTIVE, NONASSERTIVE, OR AGGRESSIVE?:

ROLE:

GOAL:

NONVERBALS:

Stress TEST levels

Rate your level of negative thought or worry:

During Situation	Overall Level for Day
|-|-|-|-|-|-|-|-|-|-|	|-|-|-|-|-|-|-|-|-|-|
0 1 2 3 4 5 6 7 8 9 10	0 1 2 3 4 5 6 7 8 9 10

Rate your level of negative emotion:

During Situation	Overall Level for Day
|-|-|-|-|-|-|-|-|-|-|	|-|-|-|-|-|-|-|-|-|-|
0 1 2 3 4 5 6 7 8 9 10	0 1 2 3 4 5 6 7 8 9 10

Rate your level of physical symptoms:

During Situation	Overall Level for Day
|-|-|-|-|-|-|-|-|-|-|	|-|-|-|-|-|-|-|-|-|-|
0 1 2 3 4 5 6 7 8 9 10	0 1 2 3 4 5 6 7 8 9 10

YOU (Rewrite if original was aggressive or nonassertive)

ASSERTIVE PROBLEM-SOLVING GOAL:

ASSERTIVE SELF-EXPRESSION GOAL:

BEHAVIOR LINE:

SPEECH LINE:

FEELING LINE:

THOUGHT LINE:

INDIVIDUAL EXERCISE 3.3:
INTERPRETING YOUR STRESS/ASSERTIVENESS DIARY

In this exercise, take a look at your Diary (Exercise 3.2). On which days did you experience the highest and lowest levels of stress? Were you more assertive on high or low stress days? Which is most likely to be stressful for you: assertiveness, aggressiveness, or nonassertiveness?

INDIVIDUAL EXERCISE 3.4:
BRAINSTORMING ALTERNATIVES

In this exercise select one problem situation from your diary. Describe it below. Then brainstorm four alternative, assertive Behavior, Thought, and Speech Lines. Complete the exercise by circling your preferred alternatives.

GENERAL SITUATION:

OTHER PERSON (If any):

    BEHAVIOR LINE:
    SPEECH LINE:

YOU (what you actually did)

    BEHAVIOR LINE:
    SPEECH LINE:
    FEELING LINE:
    THOUGHT LINE:

ASSERTIVENESS ANALYSIS

    ASSERTIVE, NONASSERTIVE, OR AGGRESSIVE:

    ROLE:

    GOAL:

    NONVERBALS:

YOU (rewritten assertively)

BEHAVIOR LINE:
SPEECH LINE:
FEELING LINE:
THOUGHT LINE:

BRAINSTORMED ALTERNATIVES

BEHAVIOR LINES:
1.
2.
3.
4.

SPEECH LINES:
1.
2.
3.
4.

THOUGHT LINES:
1.
2.
3.
4.

PROBLEM-SOLVING GOALS:
1.
2.
3.
4.

SELF-EXPRESSION GOALS:
1.
2.
3.
4.

INDIVIDUAL EXERCISE 3.5:
COSTS AND PAYOFFS

Often it is not easy to be assertive.   There are times when aggression and nonassertion have their payoffs.   In difficult situations it can be useful to weigh the costs and benefits of assertiveness before deciding what to do.   In particular, weigh the short- and long-term consequences since short-term costs can at times lead to long-term benefits.   Generally, here are some of the questions you might want to consider.   First select a problem situation in which you were nonassertive or aggressive.   Then answer the questions on the Costs and Payoffs Worksheet on the following page.   This exercise concludes with a reassessment of the general advantages and disadvantages to being assertive in the situation you described.

PROBLEM SITUATION:

YOUR BEHAVIOR LINE:

YOUR SPEECH LINE:

YOUR THOUGHT LINE:

Costs and Payoffs Worksheet

	Assertiveness	*Aggressiveness*	*Nonassertiveness*

Costs?

(Short-term)

(Long-term)

Payoffs?

(Short-term)

(Long-term)

Assertiveness: Overall Advantages and Disadvantages

Now, consider all the costs and payoffs you listed on the previous page. How important is each? Which should you take seriously. In the spaces below, list only the *important* advantages and disadvantages to being assertive in your situation. Give each a score from 0 to 10 (in which 0 = "Not at All Important" and 10 = "Extremely Important").

Advantages	Score	Disadvantages	Score

Now, add up your advantages and disadvantages scores. Which is higher?

In light of your score, what behavior, thought, and speech lines do you feel are most appropriate?

YOUR BEHAVIOR LINE:

YOUR THOUGHT LINE:

YOUR SPEECH LINE:

INDIVIDUAL EXERCISE 3.6:
ASSERTIVENESS AND DEFENSIVENESS

Attack and avoidance are often habitual and used without thought. They are not tailored to the situation. However, sometimes defensive behavior is appropriate and healthy. For example, if you were to be attacked by a wild dog in a park, the defensive strategy of running would be appropriate. Can you think of other situations when attack and avoidance might be called for? Try to develop a checklist of criteria for determining when defensive behavior might be appropriate.

Recall that the goals of defensive behavior are to protect oneself and minimize pain without actively coping. In what ways can aggressiveness and nonassertiveness be defensive?

Here is a somewhat similar question. Can you think of examples of nonassertive behavior that are also aggressive?

GROUP EXERCISE 3.7: IDENTIFYING EXAMPLES

Divide into teams of four people each. Each member selects an example developed for Individual Exercise 3.1, without labeling the type of situation it is or whether it is assertive, nonassertive, or aggressive. Remaining group members attempt to determine the type of situation and whether it is assertive, nonassertive, or aggressive. Members should explain their answers.

This exercise may be continued by having members offer assertive alternatives to nonassertive or aggressive examples. Each assertive suggestion should be explained in terms of the criteria presented in the chapter.

GROUP EXERCISE 3.8: ROLE-PLAYING

Two people select a stress situation to act out (from Individual Exercise 3.2). The remaining members sit in a circle around the actors. First, act out a nonassertive or aggressive version of the situation. The remaining team members try to identify:

What were the apparent goals of each participant?
How well were these goals reached? Why?
What SCRIPT rules were followed?
How was the situation nonassertive or aggressive?
What nonverbals were displayed?

The team then considers the assertive version. Before acting out this script, first describe the problem-solving and assertive goals.

Once these goals are discussed, the team considers the following questions:

How realistic are these goals?
What alternative goals might be equally assertive?
What are some of the possible long-term costs and payoffs of considering these and similar goals?
What are some of the possible long-term costs and payoffs of avoiding these and similar goals?

The same two members then act out the assertive script. Team member tasks include:

Identify how the role-playing is more assertive. What text criteria were successfully followed.
How might this role-playing be even more assertive? How might it be polished up?
How reasonable is this script given the stated goals?
Since there is no one way of being assertive, what alternative assertive responses are possible?

OPTIONAL RELAXATION ASSIGNMENT: YOGAFORM STRETCHING

If you are completing the relaxation program presented in Part III of this book, read Lesson 3. If you are completing the *Relaxation Dynamics* program, read Lesson 8.

Exercises for Chapter 4

INDIVIDUAL EXERCISE 4.1:
ASSERTIVENESS AND THE FOUR COPING QUESTIONS

Here are the 12 forms of people stress we discussed in Chapter 3.

1. Meeting and getting to know someone
2. Expressing positive feelings
3. Expressing sadness, fear, or anxiety
4. Expressing opinions
5. Making requests
6. Saying no
7. Negotiating
8. Standing up for yourself in impersonal situations
9. Offering negative feedback
10. Expressing anger
11. Dealing with negative feedback
12. Dealing with hostile criticism and anger

Which situation is most problematic to you? Now, select a specific example of this situation. Include the specifics--who was involved, what was said, and when and where it happened. Describe this below:

Answer the following questions with respect to this situation.

> Question 1: What are your thoughts or assumptions?   Which seems to be most important?   How true is it?
> Question 2: How is this thought or assumption stressful?
> Question 3: How is your thinking irrational or self-defeating?
> Question 4: What is your counter Thought Line?   How true is it?
> Question 5: Now, return to your original stressful thought or assumption.   Reevaluate how true it is.

Example

SITUATION: Expressing Opinions in Class

QUESTION 1: What are your thoughts or assumptions?   Which seems to be the most important?

> "I can't speak out because I might make a mistake and look like a fool.   It would be all my fault."

How true is it?   Not true |-|-|-|-|-|-|-|-|-|-| true
0 1 2 3 4 5 6 7 8 9 10

QUESTION 2: How is this thought or assumption stressful?

___ All-or-none thinking	___ Helpless thinking
X Awfulizing	X Leaping to conclusions
___ Blaming	___ Mind-reading
___ Childhood fantasy	___ Minimizing
___ Egocentrism	X Musturbating
___ Fortune-telling	X Personalizing

QUESTION 3: How is your thinking self-defeating or irrational?

> "I'm assuming that it is terrible to look bad in front of others, you must always present your best face forward.   Let's be realistic.   If I make a mistake, it can generally be corrected."

QUESTION 4: What is your counter thought line?

> "I'll speak my mind.   No real harm in trying."

How true is it?   Not true |-|-|-|-|-|-|-|-|-|-| true
0 1 2 3 4 5 6 7 8 9 10

QUESTION 5: Now, reconsider your original thought line.

How true is it? Not true |-|-|-|-|-|-|-|-|-|-|-| true
                              0 1 2 3 4 5 6 7 8 9 10

Your Example

YOUR SITUATION:

QUESTION 1: What are your thoughts or assumptions? Which seems to be the most important?

How true is it? Not true |-|-|-|-|-|-|-|-|-|-|-| true
                              0 1 2 3 4 5 6 7 8 9 10

QUESTION 2: How is this thought or assumption stressful?

__ All-or-none thinking	__ Helpless thinking
__ Awfulizing	__ Leaping to conclusions
__ Blaming	__ Mind-reading
__ Childhood fantasy	__ Minimizing
__ Egocentrism	__ Musturbating
__ Fortune-telling	__ Personalizing

QUESTION 3: How is your thinking self-defeating or irrational?

QUESTION 4: What is your counter thought line?

How true is it? Not true |-|-|-|-|-|-|-|-|-|-|-| true
                              0 1 2 3 4 5 6 7 8 9 10

QUESTION 5: Now, reconsider your original thought line.

How true is it? Not true |-|-|-|-|-|-|-|-|-|-|-| true
                              0 1 2 3 4 5 6 7 8 9 10

EXERCISE 4.2:
STRESS/ASSERTIVENESS DIARY

This week continue with your Stress/Assertiveness Diary. However, this time we focus on your Thought Lines in terms of the four coping questions. We start with an example:

GENERAL SITUATION: Telling my date I am not interested in watching his TV program

OTHER PERSON (IF ANY): My date

BEHAVIOR LINE: Comes to my place and immediately turns on TV without asking my permission.
SPEECH LINE: "Hmmm . . . this football game looks interesting."

YOU (what you actually did)

BEHAVIOR LINE: Passively sat and watched it with him.
SPEECH LINE: "Who's playing today?"
FEELING LINE: Boredom, irritation
THOUGHT LINE: "God, this is boring. It sure is rude for him to come over just to watch his shows. I would like to talk. Well, no big problem. I don't want to upset him so much he won't come over again. Maybe he'll realize how inappropriate his behavior is without me saying anything."

ASSERTIVE, NONASSERTIVE, OR AGGRESSIVE (WHY?):
Nonassertive because I didn't talk with him about my feelings.

What kinds of stress thoughts (if any) were you thinking?

___	All-or-none thinking	___	Helpless thinking
___	Awfulizing	___	Leaping to conclusions
___	Blaming	___	Mind-reading
___	Childhood fantasy	_X_	Minimizing
___	Egocentrism	___	Musturbating
_X_	Fortune-telling	___	Personalizing

If your thought line was stressful, how was it self-defeating or irrational?

I'm thinking that it's important to be liked and avoid saying things that might make you less liked. However, no one can be liked by everyone all the time. People are more likely to like and respect you if they know what you really are thinking and feeling--and trust that you'll say what you think.

What is your counter thought line (if applicable)?

"Hey, I have the right to say what's on my mind. After all, he is my guest, not my boss."

Stress TEST levels

Rate your level of negative thought or worry:

During Situation	Overall Level for Day
0 1 2 3 4 5 6 7 8 9 10	0 1 2 3 4 5 6 7 8 9 10

Rate your level of negative emotion:

During Situation	Overall Level for Day
0 1 2 3 4 5 6 7 8 9 10	0 1 2 3 4 5 6 7 8 9 10

Rate your level of physical symptoms:

During Situation	Overall Level for Day
0 1 2 3 4 5 6 7 8 9 10	0 1 2 3 4 5 6 7 8 9 10

Stress Diary: DAY _____ [Make one copy for each day of week]

GENERAL SITUATION:

OTHER PERSON (IF ANY):

BEHAVIOR LINE:
SPEECH LINE:

YOU

BEHAVIOR LINE:
SPEECH LINE:
FEELING LINE:
THOUGHT LINE:

Assertive, Nonassertive, or Aggressive (Why?):

What kinds of stress thoughts (if any) were you thinking?

___ All-or-none thinking   ___ Helpless thinking
___ Awfulizing   ___ Leaping to conclusions
___ Blaming   ___ Mind-reading
___ Childhood fantasy   ___ Minimizing
___ Egocentrism   ___ Musturbating
___ Fortune-telling   ___ Personalizing

If your thought line was stressful, how was it self-defeating or irrational?

What is your counter thought line?

Stress TEST levels

Rate your level of negative thought or worry:

During Situation	Overall Level for Day
|-|-|-|-|-|-|-|-|-|-|	|-|-|-|-|-|-|-|-|-|-|
0 1 2 3 4 5 6 7 8 9 10	0 1 2 3 4 5 6 7 8 9 10

Rate your level of negative emotion:

During Situation	Overall Level for Day
|-|-|-|-|-|-|-|-|-|-|	|-|-|-|-|-|-|-|-|-|-|
0 1 2 3 4 5 6 7 8 9 10	0 1 2 3 4 5 6 7 8 9 10

Rate your level of physical symptoms:

During Situation	Overall Level for Day
|-|-|-|-|-|-|-|-|-|-|	|-|-|-|-|-|-|-|-|-|-|
0 1 2 3 4 5 6 7 8 9 10	0 1 2 3 4 5 6 7 8 9 10

INDIVIDUAL EXERCISE 4.3:
COMPARING LOW AND HIGH STRESS SITUATIONS

In this exercise examine low and high stress situations reported in your stress diary. What differences can you see in your Thought, Behavior, and Speech Lines When were you more assertive? When was your thinking more rational and useful?

INDIVIDUAL EXERCISE 4.4:
STRESSFUL ASSUMPTIONS

Our basic assumptions explain why we think, speak, and behave the way we do. They reflect our beliefs about ourselves and the world. Thus, assumptions are more general than most stressful thoughts. This exercise presents a number of stressful thoughts. You are to think of a general belief or assumption that might explain why a person might think this way. For example:

STRESSFUL THOUGHTS:

"I must impress my girlfriend."
"If my teacher criticizes my performance, I feel like it's the end of the world."
"I just couldn't accept myself if I didn't live up to my father's expectations."

ASSUMPTION:

"Others must like and respect me before I can feel good about myself."

Here are some more for you to try:

STRESSFUL THOUGHTS:

"If I don't get an 'A,' then I might as well give up."
"I can, and must, be the best at work."
"I can never do too much for my children."

ASSUMPTION:

STRESSFUL THOUGHTS:

"All my friends seem to be better lovers than I am."
"I just can't do as well as my brother in anything."
"Whatever I turn in at work will be inferior."

ASSUMPTION:

STRESSFUL THOUGHTS:

"My work problem is so serious that I dare not let it out of my mind."
"I can't afford to take it easy. I would really get into trouble then."
"I gotta keep worrying. There has to be an answer."

ASSUMPTION:

INDIVIDUAL EXERCISE 4.5:
THE WHY QUESTION

One way of figuring out what stressful assumptions underlie our thoughts is to ask a series of Why Questions. That is, after you have identified a stressful thought, ask: "Why is this thought important or stressful for me?" Put down your answer. Then ask the question again: "Why is this thought important or stressful for me?" Continue asking the Why Question until you identify an underlying assumption for your stressful thinking. Then analyze how your assumption is irrational or self-defeating. Here's an example:

GENERAL SITUATION: Last week my coworker asked me to finish his report for him. He said he had important business to do at home.
BEHAVIOR LINE: I slammed his report on my desk and looked away.
FEELING LINE: I got really irritated and frustrated. My stomach started hurting.

THOUGHT LINE: "Boy, he's got some nerve. Always trying to take advantage of me."

WHY QUESTION: "Why is this thought important or stressful for me?"

THOUGHT LINE: "People always think I'm the one they can use. Nobody thinks of my feelings."

WHY QUESTION: "Why is this thought important or stressful for me?"

THOUGHT LINE: "It is important that people always be considerate of my feelings and respect me."

WHY QUESTION: "Why is this thought important or stressful for me?"

THOUGHT LINE: "I don't feel OK or accepted unless people respect me."

HOW IRRATIONAL OR SELF-DEFEATING: "It's silly to base my self-respect on what others think. It's impossible for everyone to like me. I'm OK because I accept myself, and that's enough."

Here's your example:

GENERAL SITUATION:

BEHAVIOR LINE:

FEELING LINE:

THOUGHT LINE:

WHY QUESTION: "Why is this thought important or stressful for me?"

THOUGHT LINE:

WHY QUESTION: "Why is this thought important or stressful for me?"

THOUGHT LINE:

WHY QUESTION: "Why is this thought important or stressful for me?"

THOUGHT LINE:

WHY IRRATIONAL OR SELF-DEFEATING:

INDIVIDUAL EXERCISE 4.6:
STRESS THINKING CAUSES STRESS THINKING

Some forms of stress thought can lead to others. Can you think of examples? For example, a person who first musturbates by thinking, "It is absolutely essential that I get that raise" would likely awfulize after not receiving a raise, "It is the end of the road that I did not get that raise."

INDIVIDUAL EXERCISE 4.7:
STRESS THINKING AND WORK

Different lines of work are more conducive to different forms of stress thinking. For example, if you are a salesperson and are entirely responsible for setting up and completing your sales, it would make sense that you might tend to personalize if a sale fell through. In contrast, if, in your line of work, assignments are always given to you by a supervisor, you might be more likely to engage in blaming. What types of stress thinking might be common where you work? Why?

INDIVIDUAL EXERCISE 4.8:
COSTS AND PAYOFFS

As with nonassertiveness and aggression, there are times when irrational and self-defeating Thought Lines can have their payoffs. In difficult situations it can be useful to weigh the costs and benefits of rational and useful thinking before deciding what to do. In particular, weigh the short and long-term consequences since short-term costs can at times lead to long-term benefits.

Generally, here are some of the questions you might want to consider. First select a problem situation in which your Thought Line was stressful, irrational, or self-defeating. Then answer the questions on the Costs and Payoffs Worksheet on the following page. This exercise concludes with a reassessment of the general advantages and disadvantages to rational and useful thinking in the situation you described.

GENERAL SITUATION:

THOUGHT LINE:

Costs and Payoffs Chart

	Rational and Useful	*Irrational and Self-Defeating*
Costs?		
(Short-term)		
(Long-term)		
Payoffs?		
(Short-term)		
(Long-term)		

Rational and Useful Thinking:
Overall Advantages and Disadvantages

Now, consider all the costs and payoffs you listed on the previous page. How important is each? Which should you take seriously. In the spaces below, list only the *important* advantages and disadvantages to being assertive in your situation. Give each a score from 0 to 10 (in which 0 = "Not at All Important" and 10 = "Extremely important").

Now, add up your advantages and disadvantages scores. Which is higher?

Considering this score, what is your revised thought line?

THOUGHT LINE:

INDIVIDUAL EXERCISE 4.9:
BRAINSTORMING ALTERNATIVE INTERPRETATIONS

It can be useful to consider our stressful thoughts and assumptions as including interpretations of a stress situation. Once we have identified how we are interpreting a situation, we can then brainstorm alternative interpretations, and select which are most adaptive and reasonable. For example, take the following situation:

OTHER PERSON: Your boss

BEHAVIOR LINE: Rushes in and slams the door to his office.
SPEECH LINE: "Get to work."

YOU:

THOUGHT LINE: "Gosh. The boss must not like me. I'm in trouble."

ALTERNATIVE INTERPRETATIONS:
1. "The boss is late and upset with himself."
2. "The boss saw me drinking a cup of coffee and incorrectly assumed I haven't done any work."
3. "The boss is in a hurry and wants us to work faster."
4. "The boss wasn't talking to me."
5. "The boss was just joking."

Which of the these alternatives seems most rational and useful to you?

> "The boss saw me drinking a cup of coffee and incorrectly assumed I haven't done any work." This is adaptive because it tells me specifically what I have to do--not take a coffee break when the boss comes in. It is rational because I was indeed drinking coffee and the boss is a hard worker."

Now, try this exercise yourself.

INDIVIDUAL EXERCISE 4.10:
THINKING THROUGH YOUR INTERPRETATIONS

This exercise involves thinking through troublesome interpretations. It simply involves asking a few key questions about it.

First, describe your stress-producing interpretation.

Here are the questions:

1. What is the evidence for your interpretation?
2. Realistically, what would be the worst consequence if your interpretation were correct?
3. How likely is this to happen?
4. In fact, how might this consequence be not as bad as you fear?
5. What is the evidence against your interpretation?
6. What are the long-term costs of continuing to hold your troublesome interpretation?
7. What are the long-term payoffs of changing your troublesome interpretation?

INDIVIDUAL EXERCISE 4.11:
TALKING TO AN IMAGINARY FRIEND

Imagine a friend has encountered the exact same stress situation you have experienced. What kinds of things would you say to this person? This exercise can be a very useful way of checking stressful thinking and assumptions. We are much more likely to be needlessly hard on ourselves. The advice we give to friends is often more rational and useful.

INDIVIDUAL EXERCISE 4.12:
THE COPING DICTIONARY

The stress dictionary lists 12 ways people often create needless stress through irrational and self-destructive thinking. For each type of stressful thinking there is a corresponding type of "coping thinking" that is rational and useful. For example, whereas "All-or-none thinking" is often stressful, "Acknowledging shades of gray" can often help one cope. Similarly, "Awfulizing" is stressful, whereas "Seeing things in perspective" is more conducive to coping. Below are the 12 types of stressful thought we considered earlier. See if you can identify and label a type of "coping thought" for each.

Stressful Thinking	Coping Thinking
All-or-none thinking	
Awfulizing	
Blaming	
Childhood fantasy	
Egocentrism	
Fortune-telling	
Helpless thinking	
Leaping to conclusions	
Mind-reading	
Minimizing	
Musturbating	
Personalizing	

GROUP EXERCISE 4.13:
DISCUSSION OF DIARIES

Divide into teams of four. Each person shares one stress situation. The goal of this exercise is for each team to reach a consensus as to:

1. The type of stress thought illustrated
2. How the thought is self-defeating or irrational
3. The basic hidden stressful assumption it represents
4. Appropriate counter thoughts

GROUP EXERCISE 4.14:
QUESTIONING AND CHALLENGING INTERPRETATIONS

Group members divide into teams of two. Each person switches roles, with one person presenting the other person's stress situation and interpretations. The other person then questions and challenges these interpretations.

OPTIONAL RELAXATION ASSIGNMENT:
BREATHING EXERCISES

If you are completing the relaxation program presented at the end of this book, read Lesson 4. If you are completing the *Relaxation Dynamics* program, complete Lesson 9.

Exercises for Chapter 5

EXERCISE 5.1:
EXAMPLES OF CUES

Cues can be environmental stimuli, behaviors, thoughts, feelings, or speech. See if you can think of examples of each in your own life. Here are some examples to get you going.

Environmental Stimulus Cues

Your first work task each day is report to your supervisor on your past day's activities. This creates considerable anxiety. The anxiety begins in the pre-stress phase, usually when you are riding the bus to work. You decide to use the approaching bus as an environmental cue, a signal to begin practicing your relaxation exercises and think, "Now, it won't be that bad. After 30 minutes it will be all over and I can enjoy the rest of the day."

You experience a considerable degree of pressure at work. Right about 1 P.M. you start feeling it, usually with a headache. You decide to use the noon hour chime as a cue to sit back and relax deeply for 10 minutes. During this period you think, "One thing at a time. The day's half over."

Your examples:

Behavioral Cues

You're at a meeting. The person you sit next to often upsets you so much that you become inappropriately hostile. The moment he begins talking, you think, "Take it easy. Let this person speak. I may not agree with his views, but he should have a chance to say them."

You're waiting to take a test. The instructor begins to distribute the exams. The moment you close your book you think, "I close my book. That's my cue to take a deep breath and relax. Answer one question at a time."

Your examples:

Thought Cues

You are at a party and want to meet the attractive person standing alone at the other end of the room At first you think, "They'll never talk to me. I've got nothing to offer." Your next thought is, "Thinking negative--that's my cue to make up my mind and act. I'll just introduce myself. No harm in that."

You are standing in line and someone has unexpectedly bumped you. You think, "That bum. Trying to push ahead. Wait till I give that person a piece of my mind." Then you think, "Blaming--that's my cue to pause, count to ten, and decide on the most reasonable course of action."

Your examples:

Feeling Cues

You are at an important meeting. Each person has to give a report. Your turn is coming up and you begin to feel jittery and sick in the stomach. You think, "My stomach is beginning to feel upset. This is my cue to do a few deep breathing exercises."

Your secretary often annoys you by talking about trivia. Today he begins to talk about how wonderful his children are. You begin to feel angry. You think "Anger--my cue to sit back and relax. This is going to upset me, but I know how to deal with it."

Your examples:

Speech Cues

You and your spouse are spending the evening together. Unexpectedly, she brings up the topic of how to spend the upcoming holiday weekend. She says, "Let's take a drive to the country." You think, "She brings up a discussion question. That's my cue not to passively give in, but offer my own suggestions."

You are cleaning the yard and want your son to help. He complains, "Oh, no, do I really have to?" You begin to say, "Well, maybe not." You think "I'm giving in. That's my cue to pause, and repeat my request, and not give in."

Your examples:

INDIVIDUAL EXERCISE 5.2: STRESS DIARY

This week we will continue with our stress diaries. However, this time identify whether the situation is a pre-stress, mid-stress, or post-stress situation. Circle which are appropriate. Also, we have added a space for you to describe your stress cues indicating when you should take action. Finally, indicate your completion thoughts. As before, describe *actual stress events* rather than wished-for outcomes.

Your Stress Diary: EXAMPLE

TYPE OF SITUATION
(PRE-STRESS, MID-STRESS, POST-STRESS)

> DESCRIBE SITUATION: I was waiting for my supervisor to meet with me to give me feedback on my performance over the last six months.

> WHAT MADE IT A STRESS SITUATION? I really got anxious. My feelings included fear and anxiety. I awfulized and engaged in negative, personalized thinking. My Thought Lines included, "I'll bet I did terribly. I'm going to be so embarrassed. He's going to comment on every time I came in a little late. It's all my fault people aren't working as hard as they should."

> CUE: Every time my supervisor mentions the upcoming review, I begin to feel anxious. This would be a good time to think of using my coping skills.

YOUR COPING RESPONSE

> BEHAVIOR LINE (INCLUDING RELAXATION AND ASSERTIVE RESPONSES): I take a deep breath and do a brief relaxation exercise. I try to divert my attention from my supervisor's desk by looking down at my papers.

> SPEECH LINE: I say nothing.

> THOUGHT LINE: "This review will be a good opportunity for me to learn from my mistakes. I know that there is no way I could have done any worse than anyone else. Besides, if I were really doing badly, they would have let me know by now."

> COMPLETION THOUGHT: "Good. It's over with."

Stress TEST levels

Rate your level of negative thought or worry:

During Situation	Overall Level for Day
⊦-⊦-⊦-⊦-⊦-|-|-|-|-|-|	⊦-⊦-⊦-⊦-⊦-|-|-|-|-|-|
0 1 2 3 4 5 6 7 8 9 10	0 1 2 3 4 5 6 7 8 9 10

Rate your level of negative emotion:

During Situation	Overall Level for Day
|-|-|-|-|-|-|-|-|-|-|	|-|-|-|-|-|-|-|-|-|-|
0 1 2 3 4 5 6 7 8 9 10	0 1 2 3 4 5 6 7 8 9 10

Rate your level of physical symptoms:

During Situation	Overall Level for Day
|-|-|-|-|-|-|-|-|-|-|	|-|-|-|-|-|-|-|-|-|-|
0 1 2 3 4 5 6 7 8 9 10	0 1 2 3 4 5 6 7 8 9 10

Your Stress Diary: Day ___

TYPE OF SITUATION
(PRE-STRESS, MID-STRESS, POST-STRESS)

DESCRIBE SITUATION:

WHAT MADE IT A STRESS SITUATION?

CUE:

YOUR COPING RESPONSE:

BEHAVIOR   LINE   (INCLUDING   RELAXATION   AND
ASSERTIVE RESPONSES):

SPEECH LINE:

THOUGHT LINE:

COMPLETION THOUGHT:

Stress TEST levels

Rate your level of negative thought or worry:

During Situation	Overall Level for Day
|-|-|-|-|-|-|-|-|-|-|	|-|-|-|-|-|-|-|-|-|-|
0 1 2 3 4 5 6 7 8 9 10	0 1 2 3 4 5 6 7 8 9 10

Rate your level of negative emotion:

During Situation	Overall Level for Day
|-|-|-|-|-|-|-|-|-|-|	|-|-|-|-|-|-|-|-|-|-|
0 1 2 3 4 5 6 7 8 9 10	0 1 2 3 4 5 6 7 8 9 10

Rate your level of physical symptoms:

During Situation	Overall Level for Day
|-|-|-|-|-|-|-|-|-|-|	|-|-|-|-|-|-|-|-|-|-|
0 1 2 3 4 5 6 7 8 9 10	0 1 2 3 4 5 6 7 8 9 10

INDIVIDUAL EXERCISE 5.3:
BRAINSTORMING CUES

In this exercise select one stress situation you reported in your diary. Then take a look at the cue you have identified. Brainstorm four additional cues.

TYPE OF SITUATION
(PRE-STRESS, MID-STRESS, POST-STRESS):

DESCRIBE SITUATION:

WHAT WENT WRONG?   WHAT MADE IT A STRESS SITUATION?

ALTERNATIVE CUES
    1.
    2.
    3.
    4.

Circle your best alternative

GROUP EXERCISE 5.4:
STRESS CUES

Divide into teams of eight (if possible). Each team is to think of a real-life example of pre-stress, mid-stress, and post-stress. Identify the goals and cues for each example.

OPTIONAL RELAXATION ASSIGNMENT:
THEMATIC IMAGERY

If you are completing the relaxation program at the end of this book, complete Lesson 5. If you are completing the *Relaxation Dynamics* program, read Lessons 10 and 11.

Exercises for Chapter 6

INDIVIDUAL EXERCISE 6.1:
THE CONTRACT

Let's consider a contract for the remainder of this book. Six additional chapters are included in Part 2. What rewards will you present yourself for completing them in the time indicated?

Goal	Time	Reward
Chapters 7-8		
Chapter 9		
Chapter 10		
Chapter 11		
Chapter 12		

Are you ready to sign? Here's the contract.

I, _____, HEREBY CONTRACT TO COMPLETE _____ (NUMBER OF CHAPTERS). UPON COMPLETING THIS NUMBER AT THE TIME INDICATED, I HEREBY AGREE TO GIVE MYSELF THE REWARD DESCRIBED.

SIGNATURE: _____ DATE: _____

INDIVIDUAL EXERCISE 6.2:
RESISTANT THINKING

What types of resistant thinking interfere with your efforts to deal with stress more effectively?

For each type of resistant thinking, state a rational and useful counter.

GROUP EXERCISE 6.3:
EVALUATING CONTRACTS

Each person begins by writing a practice contract for a realistic coping task. It can involve being assertive or thinking in a rational and useful way in a specific situation. This contract is just for practice, you don't have to carry it out.

Then divide into teams of four. Compare contracts. When each person presents a contract, other members evaluate how appropriate and realistic the goals and rewards are using the rules presented in Chapter 6.

OPTIONAL RELAXATION ASSIGNMENT:
MEDITATION

If you are completing the relaxation program at the end of this book, complete Lesson 6. If you are completing the *Relaxation Dynamics* program, read Lessons 12, 13, and 14.

Exercises for Chapter 7

INDIVIDUAL EXERCISE 7.1:
SIMPLE FACTS

EXERCISE CONTRACT

I, _____, HEREBY
CONTRACT WITH MYSELF TO COMPLETE THE FOLLOWING
EXERCISE. IF I FINISH BY THE FOLLOWING DATE,
_____, I WILL GIVE MYSELF THIS REWARD:
_____

SIGNATURE: _____ DATE: _____

In the segments below are a variety of scripts. We begin with a few poorly written script lines and violate our SCRIPT rules.

> GENERAL SITUATION: Joan has asked her husband, Will, to take the garbage out several times this week. She dislikes having to do this heavy work all by herself and would like Will to do some of it without her asking.
>
> DESCRIBE: "Why do I have to do all the work around here? Why don't you pitch in and do some of it?"
>
> EXPRESS/INTERPRET: "I'm at my wit's end. If you don't carry your weight around here, I'm going to have to do something."
>
> REQUEST: "Is this really asking too much? Here's the garbage. Now, why don't you be nice and take it out."
>
> CONSEQUENCES: "You should do your share of the work."

<u>NO</u> Simple
<u>NO</u> Concrete
<u>NO</u> Realistic
___ Important
___ Personal
___ Timely

This script gets a low SCRIPT score. None of Joan's statements get to the actual concrete facts of the matter. Her Describe statement doesn't state what the problem behavior is. We cannot tell from her Express statement what her real feelings are. Indeed, her Express statement includes a threat which doesn't even belong there. Generally, her statements are vague, emotional, and overstated outbursts. Here's an improved version:

DESCRIBE: "Will, this week I took the garbage out on Sunday, Tuesday, and Wednesday, even though I asked you to do it."

EXPRESS/INTERPRET: "I am getting pissed off at having to take the garbage out, and getting no response to my requests. I think it is only fair that we should share the work, but you don't seem to be cooperating."

REQUEST: "Please help me out today to take the garbage out."

CONSEQUENCES: "If we can get the job done, I'll have more time to do my work and won' have to keep bugging you."

Here's another script to evaluate:

GENERAL SITUATION: Gretchen is the chief nursing supervisor in a small hospital. Bill has just started work as a nurse and is making a few mistakes. Most often, he forgets to refile patient record folders.

DESCRIBE: "Bill, you're doing a good job. But you should really try to be more diligent about your schedule. For quite some time, your work just hasn't been good enough."

EXPRESS/INTERPRET: "Things just aren't as tightly run as they should be."

REQUEST: "Try to do your job more carefully in the future, OK?"

CONSEQUENCES: "I really don't want to seem like I'm bothering you. I know you are really trying."

<u>*NO*</u> *Simple*
<u>*NO*</u> *Concrete*
<u>*NO*</u> *Realistic*
___ *Important*
___ *Personal*
___ *Timely*

First, these statements do not follow the rules of what to include. The Describe statement says nothing specific about Bill's behavior. The Express/Interpret statement does not express a thought or feeling and the Consequences statement does not present consequences. The Request is vague and abstract. Here's a better version.

DESCRIBE: "Bill, patient record files are confidential. When you are finished writing a report, please return the file to the cabinet and lock it. Last Tuesday and Wednesday I found three of your patient's files on the work table. I had to refile them."

EXPRESS/INTERPRET: "I was a little startled and concerned when I noticed you weren't doing this."

REQUEST: "Starting this week, please refile a file immediately after you are finished with it."

CONSEQUENCES: "This way I can be sure it gets done and you won't have to worry about a possible reprimand from the head nurse if a file gets lost."

Now try your hand at rewriting some problematic scripts:

GENERAL SITUATION: Jake's 12-year old daughter, Bessy, has been spending Saturday nights away from home without letting her parents know where she's going.

DESCRIBE: "Bessy, I'm afraid of the trouble you might get into. Didn't I tell you never to go out without talking to me first?"

EXPRESS/INTERPRET: "You're out of line. Shape up."

REQUEST: "If you don't straighten up, you're going to get it!"

CONSEQUENCES: "Understand?"

___ *Simple*
___ *Concrete*
___ *Realistic*
___ *Important*
___ *Personal*
___ *Timely*

Your version:

DESCRIBE:
EXPRESS/INTERPRET:
REQUEST:
CONSEQUENCES:

Now let's consider Bessy's side of the problem.

GENERAL SITUATION: Bessy has asked her parents permission to stay out three times. Each time they have refused.

DESCRIBE: "You never treat me like an adult or let me do what I want."

EXPRESS/INTERPRET: "I'm old enough. Everyone else is going out, and I can't. I don't think you care for me at all."

REQUEST: "Please don't treat me like a kid anymore."

CONSEQUENCES: "I just can't stand this any more."

       ___ *Simple*
       ___ *Concrete*
       ___ *Realistic*
       ___ *Important*
       ___ *Personal*
       ___ *Timely*

Your version:

DESCRIBE:

EXPRESS:

REQUEST:

CONSEQUENCES:

INDIVIDUAL EXERCISE 7.2:
BRAINSTORMING DERC SCRIPTS

EXERCISE CONTRACT

I, _____, HEREBY CONTRACT WITH MYSELF TO COMPLETE THE FOLLOWING EXERCISE. IF I FINISH BY THE FOLLOWING DATE, _____, I WILL GIVE MYSELF THIS REWARD:

_____

SIGNATURE: _____ DATE: _____

This exercise is a variant of the "brainstorming alternatives" exercise presented earlier. Describe a stress situation and construct a basic DERC script for dealing with it. After constructing your script, consider the possible impact it will have on others. All other components of this exercise (identifying cues, goals, the speech and behavior of the other person) are the same as in previous exercises. We begin with an example.

Example

GENERAL SITUATION: You enjoy talking with Billy, but he has a problem with not knowing when to stop talking. When you are in a conversation he goes on and on, not giving you a chance to participate.

OTHER PERSON: Billy

> SPEECH: "Last week I took this nice drive to the country and (etc., etc., etc.)
> BEHAVIOR: Stands facing you, talking with some degree of enthusiasm.

YOU

> CUE: Billy pauses to take a breath.
> PROBLEM-SOLVING GOAL: To have more "give and take" in conversations with Billy.
> SELF-EXPRESSION GOAL: To let Billy know how you feel about his monopolizing the conversation.
> ASSERTIVENESS SCRIPT:
> > DESCRIBE: "Billy, I notice we've been talking for about 20 minutes and I haven't had a chance to say a thing."

> EXPRESS/INTERPRET: "This really frustrates me. I like hearing your ideas, but I would like to share mine too, and get your feedback."
> REQUEST: "I would like to tell you about my week also."
> CONSEQUENCES: "If we could have more "give and take" in our discussions, I would enjoy it a lot more, and you would get to know more about me.

POSSIBLE REACTION: Billy might feel a bit hurt, at first. But he should realize that I'm his friend and don't want to hurt him, but develop our friendship more. I'm willing to talk about his reaction if necessary.

Your Script

GENERAL SITUATION:

OTHER PERSON:

> SPEECH:
> BEHAVIOR:

YOU

> CUE:
> PROBLEM-SOLVING GOAL:
> SELF-EXPRESSION GOAL:
> ASSERTIVENESS SCRIPT:
> > DESCRIBE STATEMENT:
> > EXPRESS/INTERPRET STATEMENT:
> > REQUEST STATEMENT:
> > CONSEQUENCES STATEMENT:

POSSIBLE REACTION:

Alternative Script #1 for Previous Situation

GENERAL SITUATION:

OTHER PERSON:

> SPEECH:
> BEHAVIOR:

YOU

    CUE:
    PROBLEM-SOLVING GOAL:
    SELF-EXPRESSION GOAL:
    ASSERTIVENESS SCRIPT:
      DESCRIBE STATEMENT:
      EXPRESS/INTERPRET STATEMENT:
      REQUEST STATEMENT:
      CONSEQUENCES STATEMENT:

POSSIBLE REACTION:

GROUP EXERCISE 7.3:
EVALUATING STATEMENTS AND SCRIPTS

As preparation for this exercise each person individually generates an example for all of the following:

Describe Statement
Express Statement
Interpret Statement
Request Statement
Consequences Statement
Impact Script
Empathic Script
Clarification Script
Contradiction Script

Each person randomly selects one example to read. The person to their right tries to determine what type of statement and/or script it illustrates. The rest of the group discusses the response. Then the person to the right evaluates the extent to which the example follows the SCRIPT rules. Again, the rest of the group discusses the response. When finished, the person to the right presents his or her example, and the next person rates it. Continue until everyone has presented an example.

GROUP EXERCISE 7.4:
EVALUATING DERC SCRIPTS

Form groups of four. Each person takes a turn presenting their DERC scripts. Other groups provide constructive feedback concerning these questions:

Do Describe, Express, Request, and Consequences lines contain the appropriate content?
Are the SCRIPT rules met?

OPTIONAL RELAXATION ASSIGNMENT:
DEVELOPING YOUR OWN RELAXATION SEQUENCE

If you are completing the relaxation program in this book, do Lesson 7.

If you are completing the *Relaxation Dynamics* program, complete *Relaxation Dynamics* Worksheet 19 (pp. 339-343).

Exercises for Chapter 8

INDIVIDUAL EXERCISE 8.1:
PROBLEM-SOLVING: THE CAT DOLL

EXERCISE CONTRACT

I, _____, HEREBY CONTRACT WITH MYSELF TO COMPLETE THE FOLLOWING EXERCISE. IF I FINISH BY THE FOLLOWING DATE, _____, I WILL GIVE MYSELF THIS REWARD:

_____

SIGNATURE: _____ DATE: _____

In this exercise, use the problem-solving strategies presented to come up with a solution. Follow each step carefully.

You are the director of a small toy manufacturing company. Your business is in serious trouble. Sales are not good. You have no money left for major investments. Your one major project, the "Moco Cat Doll," started to sell well, and then peaked. You have invested considerable money in this product and think it still has some potential. Here's the product description:

The Moco Cat Doll is essentially a cloth stuffed cat. Its skin is brown cotton fabric with nose, eyes, and whiskers painted on. The entire doll is stuffed with soft foam. Dimensions are 6 inches height and 9 inches length.

Here is how you have marketed the product in the past:

We approached J-Mart, a local discount chain, and they agreed to carry the doll.

Your problem is this: How can you redesign the Moco Cat Doll to make it more interesting and fun to play with? How can you improve the sales of this product?

INDIVIDUAL EXERCISE 8.2:
PROBLEM-SOLVING: A PERSONAL PROBLEM

EXERCISE CONTRACT

I, _____, HEREBY CONTRACT WITH MYSELF TO COMPLETE THE FOLLOWING EXERCISE. IF I FINISH BY THE FOLLOWING DATE, _____, I WILL GIVE MYSELF THIS REWARD:

_____
SIGNATURE: _____ *DATE:* _____

Think of a difficult job stress situation you have encountered this year. Using this situation, complete each step of the problem-solving procedures described in this chapter.

GROUP EXERCISE 8.3:
NEGOTIATING A SURVIVAL PLAN

Divide into two teams (any number each). In this task, both teams negotiate a solution to the following hypothetical problem. Before beginning negotiations, each team should meet separately and use the problem-solving strategies discussed in this chapter to develop a survival plan. Both teams then meet and, using the survival plan described, attempt to arrive at a solution. At the end of the exercise, discuss which text strategies worked, and which might be improved.

Two ships have crashed on opposite ends of an isolated, tropical island. The problem is indeed serious. After the ships were abandoned, they floated 100 feet out to sea and sank. Each ship was entirely under water, with only their smokestacks above water. Food supplies (enough for one month), a flashlight, and a radio were recovered. The island is five miles in diameter and

100 miles from a popular mainland resort. It is covered with coconut trees and various forms of unfamiliar and potentially poisonous berry and nut-bearing plants. Although there are no human inhabitants, a handful of small (and cute) koala bears--an endangered species--run about. In addition, there are a variety of large poisonous snakes and numerous insects. The island is covered with caves.

Each team plays the part of one group of survivors. For the first 30 minutes, each team develops a survival plan, using the problem-solving strategies described in Chapter 8. However, different survivors have differing goals, requiring some negotiation.

Before starting this exercise, select which of the following members you wish to take (gender changes are permitted):

Tidy Tina: Tina is very wealthy, and well-dressed. Her main concern is not to soil her expensive clothes, or lose her expensive jewelry.

Business Bill: Bill is always looking how to get ahead. If he can make a buck, he'll try.

Lonely Lola: Lola's main concern in life is not to be alone, even for a minute. She always wants to be with people, have friends, and look for a possible mate.

Sick Sam: Sam has broken his leg. He wants to help, but has to be careful.

Safety Sue: Sue is easily frightened. Darkness, new places, insects, strange sounds--all terrify her. In addition, she always likes to play it safe. Even small risks can create panic in her.

Go Slow Gary: His motto is "Take your time . . . what's the hurry?" Gary, a bit lazy, sees no reason to rush into anything. An eternal optimist, he figures that things always work out, and the less done, the better.

Then both teams meet (for the first time). The task becomes one of negotiation. What survival plan should the entire group of survivors use?

When you are finished, the entire group considers the following questions:

What negotiation strategies mentioned in the book were used?

What strategies were not used? Why?

Using the ideas presented in this book, how might the negotiations have been improved?

GROUP EXERCISE 8.4:
NEGOTIATING A REAL-LIFE PROBLEM

Divide into teams of four. Each team selects one real-life example of negotiation that was somewhat less than effective. Using the points presented in this chapter, the team tries to identify how the negotiation could have been improved. When finished, each team presents the details (without analysis or evaluation) of the negotiation situation to the other team. The other team tries to evaluate it and determine what went wrong.

OPTIONAL RELAXATION ASSIGNMENT:
THE MINI-RELAXATION

Complete relaxation Lesson 8 at the end of this book. This lesson is for those who are completing the relaxation program in this book as well as for those who are completing the *Relaxation Dynamics* program.

Exercises for Chapter 9

INDIVIDUAL EXERCISE 9.1:
DEALING WITH SABOTAGE

EXERCISE CONTRACT

I, _____, HEREBY
CONTRACT WITH MYSELF TO COMPLETE THE FOLLOWING
EXERCISE. IF I FINISH BY THE FOLLOWING DATE,
_____, I WILL GIVE MYSELF THIS REWARD:
_____
SIGNATURE: _____ DATE: _____

First select a stress situation in which you actually had a sensible coping strategy, but it didn't work quite as well as you had hoped.

GENERAL SITUATION:

OTHER PERSON:

> SPEECH LINE:
> BEHAVIOR LINE:

YOU

> CUE:
> PROBLEM-SOLVING GOAL:
> SELF-EXPRESSION GOAL:
> ASSERTIVENESS SCRIPT:

WHAT WENT WRONG?:

   SELF-SABOTAGE:

   COUNTER THOUGHT:

   SABOTAGE FROM OTHERS:

   COUNTER SCRIPT:

GROUP EXERCISE 9.2:
IDENTIFYING SABOTAGE FROM OTHERS

   In responding to sabotage from others, it is first useful to recognize when it is occurring. In running stress groups, I have often used an exercise that is a variant of the popular Trivia game. In Trivia, as you recall, one person reads a statement, perhaps a well-known line from a famous movie. You have to identify the statement. (For example, you might be asked "What popular TV sergeant said 'Just the facts, ma'am'"?) In my version, one person reads a sabotaging statement, while the other tries to identify what type it is.

   Divide into groups of four. One person faces the person to the right and reads one of the following sabotaging statements. The listener then attempts to identify what type of sabotage it is. The rest of the group can help. Once identified, the listener attempts an effective response.

Sabotaging Statements

"Why bother me? It's your problem. Deal with it."

TYPE OF SABOTAGE:

"You complain about no one letting you speak at the meeting. Well, you had plenty of chances to make your views known. Why didn't you talk to the committee chair before the meeting, or send us a letter of your concerns?"

TYPE OF SABOTAGE:

"You male chauvinist pig."

TYPE OF SABOTAGE:

"You know, I've been thinking about what you've just said. I couldn't agree more. I was really all in the wrong this time. Won't happen again."

TYPE OF SABOTAGE:

"I didn't clean your shirts as promised? I just thought you look better in spots."

TYPE OF SABOTAGE:

"Hey, you accuse me of being 'indifferent' to your need for clear and honest communication. Well, just what is a need? Maybe what you consider a 'need' is just a 'want.'"

TYPE OF SABOTAGE:

"Sure I borrowed your radio. It's only a radio."

TYPE OF SABOTAGE:

"I know you wanted me to call John and ask for his advice concerning our company project. What good is his input anyway? He doesn't now what's going on."

TYPE OF SABOTAGE:

"You're upset with my typing. Does this mean we aren't going out to dinner tonight?"

TYPE OF SABOTAGE:

"I guess I just don't know how to say things right without making a mess."

TYPE OF SABOTAGE:

"Ah-ha, you're being assertive! You must be taking an assertiveness course. Good practice--keep it up."

TYPE OF SABOTAGE:

"Yes, you have problems with my typing. Let me finish. I was talking to my mother and she said something you just wouldn't believe. She and the grandparents are going alone to the lake. And let me tell you what happened."

TYPE OF SABOTAGE:

"Fine, tell the boss about my coming late. I'm sure he'll love to hear about your long phone conversations with friends."

TYPE OF SABOTAGE:

"I'm the one who always has to correct your problems. You have no right to complain."

TYPE OF SABOTAGE:

"Why are you always out to get me? It just isn't fair"

TYPE OF SABOTAGE:

"I know what I said upset you. I guess I'm just no good as a parent. It's so hard these days."

TYPE OF SABOTAGE:

"Let's not discuss this vacation any more. If it's so much trouble for you to pay your share, I'll pay for the whole thing. Oh, it's nothing."

TYPE OF SABOTAGE:

GROUP EXERCISE 9.3:
RESPONDING TO SABOTAGE FROM OTHERS

Divide into teams of four. Imagine you are going to be giving advice on a radio talk show on dealing with interpersonal sabotage. As preparation, try to develop a catalogue of general sabotage-countering strategies. Make sure your strategies are general and effective enough to be useful to a large number of people. This is a problem-solving exercise.

At the end of the exercise, each team shares strategies with the other team.

GROUP EXERCISE 9.4: DERC SCRIPTS

As preparation, each person constructs one DERC script. Divide into two teams. First review all the DERC scripts and select one to work on. Team members then familiarize themselves with the stress situation described and each script line. Then, teams move to different rooms or opposite corners of the room. The task of one team is to think of a set of sabotage statements for each script line. The task of the other team is to imagine what sabotage statements might be presented, and to develop possible counters. When both pairs have developed their sabotage and counters, they act out the script. One pair presents each script line, the other attempts a sabotage, the original pair counters, and so on.

When the exercise is finished, the entire team discusses the exercise, considering these points:

What forms of sabotage were employed?
Which were most effective?
What forms of counters were used?
Which were effective?
What kinds of feelings (in each pair) did sabotage evoke?
What kinds of feelings (in each pair) did the counters evoke?

OPTIONAL RELAXATION ASSIGNMENT:
YOUR RELAXATION PHILOSOPHY

Complete relaxation Lesson 9 at the end of this book. This lesson is for those who are completing the relaxation program in this book as well as for those who are completing the *Relaxation Dynamics* program.

Exercises for Chapter 10

GROUP EXERCISE 10.1:
PAIN MANAGEMENT, BURNOUT, AND RELAPSE

The entire group shares examples of employing the strategies suggested in this chapter.   Other members discuss what type of strategy was used, and whether assertiveness could have been used.

Exercises for Chapter 11

INDIVIDUAL EXERCISE 11.1:
PUTTING SCRIPTING INTO PRACTICE:

Each attempt at dealing with stress involves taking three measures. First rate your level of stress before the situation. If you are attempting mental practice or role-playing, rate your level of stress just before practicing. Then rate your realistically desired level of stress at the end of the situation. This *target level* is your goal. In determining your goal, remember that it is often unrealistic to expect a complete absence of stress. Work for a reasonable reduction. After defining your goal, do your practice and record the actual level of stress at the end of the situation. If your actual level of stress is at or below your goal, consider the practice session a success.

To illustrate, let's start with Situation #10 (see ten-step path in Chapter 11), the easiest, "Sitting with the boss at lunch engaging in small talk." Here is my stress-level just before lunch:

Stressful Thinking Level	Stressful Emotion Level	Stressful Symptom Level
|:|:|:|:|:|:|:|:|:|:|-|	|:|:|:|:|:|:|:|-|-|-|	|:|:|:|:|:|-|-|-|-|-|
0 1 2 3 4 5 6 7 8 9 10	0 1 2 3 4 5 6 7 8 9 10	0 1 2 3 4 5 6 7 8 9 10

Here is my target level:

Stressful Thinking Level	Stressful Emotion Level	Stressful Symptom Level
|:|:|:|-|-|-|-|-|-|-|	|:|:|:|-|-|-|-|-|-|-|	|:|:|-|-|-|-|-|-|-|-|
0 1 2 3 4 5 6 7 8 9 10	0 1 2 3 4 5 6 7 8 9 10	0 1 2 3 4 5 6 7 8 9 10

I try one complete mental practice of this situation, and my stress level at the end is:

Stressful Thinking Level	Stressful Emotion Level	Stressful Symptom Level
|-|-|-|-|-|-|-|-|-|-|	|-|-|-|-|-|-|-|-|-|-|	|-|-|-|-|-|-|-|-|-|-|
0 1 2 3 4 5 6 7 8 9 10	0 1 2 3 4 5 6 7 8 9 10	0 1 2 3 4 5 6 7 8 9 10

I haven't quite met my target level. Although my levels of stressful thinking and emotion are lower than my target, I still need to try to reduce my level of stress symptoms. I need to try a few more complete mental practices before I can continue with Situation #9.

I, _____, HEREBY CONTRACT WITH MYSELF TO COMPLETE THE FOLLOWING EXERCISE. I WILL GIVE MYSELF THE FOLLOWING REWARDS IF I COMPLETE THE FOLLOWING STEPS BY THE INDICATED DATES.
SIGNATURE: _____

Situation	Date	Reward
1 (Most difficult/stressful)		
2		
3		
4		
5		
6		
7		
8		
9		
10 (Least difficult/stressful)		

Your Stress Hierarchy

(Make 10 copies of the following form, one for each situation on your hierarchy. Start with Situation #10.)

SITUATION #___

FIRST MENTAL PRACTICE (repeat until target is achieved)

Before

Stressful Thinking Level	Stressful Emotion Level	Stressful Symptom Level
|-|-|-|-|-|-|-|-|-|-|	|-|-|-|-|-|-|-|-|-|-|	|-|-|-|-|-|-|-|-|-|-|
0 1 2 3 4 5 6 7 8 9 10	0 1 2 3 4 5 6 7 8 9 10	0 1 2 3 4 5 6 7 8 9 10

Targeted

Stressful Thinking Level	Stressful Emotion Level	Stressful Symptom Level
|-|-|-|-|-|-|-|-|-|-|	|-|-|-|-|-|-|-|-|-|-|	|-|-|-|-|-|-|-|-|-|-|
0 1 2 3 4 5 6 7 8 9 10	0 1 2 3 4 5 6 7 8 9 10	0 1 2 3 4 5 6 7 8 9 10

Achieved

Stressful Thinking Level	Stressful Emotion Level	Stressful Symptom Level
|-|-|-|-|-|-|-|-|-|-|	|-|-|-|-|-|-|-|-|-|-|	|-|-|-|-|-|-|-|-|-|-|
0 1 2 3 4 5 6 7 8 9 10	0 1 2 3 4 5 6 7 8 9 10	0 1 2 3 4 5 6 7 8 9 10

SECOND MENTAL PRACTICE

Before

Stressful Thinking Level	Stressful Emotion Level	Stressful Symptom Level
|-|-|-|-|-|-|-|-|-|-|	|-|-|-|-|-|-|-|-|-|-|	|-|-|-|-|-|-|-|-|-|-|
0 1 2 3 4 5 6 7 8 9 10	0 1 2 3 4 5 6 7 8 9 10	0 1 2 3 4 5 6 7 8 9 10

Targeted

Stressful Thinking Level	Stressful Emotion Level	Stressful Symptom Level
|-|-|-|-|-|-|-|-|-|-|	|-|-|-|-|-|-|-|-|-|-|	|-|-|-|-|-|-|-|-|-|-|
0 1 2 3 4 5 6 7 8 9 10	0 1 2 3 4 5 6 7 8 9 10	0 1 2 3 4 5 6 7 8 9 10

Achieved

Stressful Thinking Level	Stressful Emotion Level	Stressful Symptom Level
|-|-|-|-|-|-|-|-|-|-|	|-|-|-|-|-|-|-|-|-|-|	|-|-|-|-|-|-|-|-|-|-|
0 1 2 3 4 5 6 7 8 9 10	0 1 2 3 4 5 6 7 8 9 10	0 1 2 3 4 5 6 7 8 9 10

THIRD MENTAL PRACTICE

Before

Stressful Thinking Level	Stressful Emotion Level	Stressful Symptom Level
|-|-|-|-|-|-|-|-|-|-|	|-|-|-|-|-|-|-|-|-|-|	|-|-|-|-|-|-|-|-|-|-|
0 1 2 3 4 5 6 7 8 9 10	0 1 2 3 4 5 6 7 8 9 10	0 1 2 3 4 5 6 7 8 9 10

Targeted

Stressful Thinking Level	Stressful Emotion Level	Stressful Symptom Level
|-|-|-|-|-|-|-|-|-|-|	|-|-|-|-|-|-|-|-|-|-|	|-|-|-|-|-|-|-|-|-|-|
0 1 2 3 4 5 6 7 8 9 10	0 1 2 3 4 5 6 7 8 9 10	0 1 2 3 4 5 6 7 8 9 10

Achieved

Stressful Thinking Level	Stressful Emotion Level	Stressful Symptom Level
|-|-|-|-|-|-|-|-|-|-|	|-|-|-|-|-|-|-|-|-|-|	|-|-|-|-|-|-|-|-|-|-|
0 1 2 3 4 5 6 7 8 9 10	0 1 2 3 4 5 6 7 8 9 10	0 1 2 3 4 5 6 7 8 9 10

ROLE-PLAYING

Before

Stressful Thinking Level	Stressful Emotion Level	Stressful Symptom Level
|-|-|-|-|-|-|-|-|-|-|	|-|-|-|-|-|-|-|-|-|-|	|-|-|-|-|-|-|-|-|-|-|
0 1 2 3 4 5 6 7 8 9 10	0 1 2 3 4 5 6 7 8 9 10	0 1 2 3 4 5 6 7 8 9 10

Targeted

Stressful Thinking Level	Stressful Emotion Level	Stressful Symptom Level
|-|-|-|-|-|-|-|-|-|-|	|-|-|-|-|-|-|-|-|-|-|	|-|-|-|-|-|-|-|-|-|-|
0 1 2 3 4 5 6 7 8 9 10	0 1 2 3 4 5 6 7 8 9 10	0 1 2 3 4 5 6 7 8 9 10

Achieved

Stressful Thinking Level	Stressful Emotion Level	Stressful Symptom Level
|-|-|-|-|-|-|-|-|-|-|	|-|-|-|-|-|-|-|-|-|-|	|-|-|-|-|-|-|-|-|-|-|
0 1 2 3 4 5 6 7 8 9 10	0 1 2 3 4 5 6 7 8 9 10	0 1 2 3 4 5 6 7 8 9 10

ACTIVE PRACTICE

Before

Stressful Thinking Level	Stressful Emotion Level	Stressful Symptom Level
|-|-|-|-|-|-|-|-|-|-|	|-|-|-|-|-|-|-|-|-|-|	|-|-|-|-|-|-|-|-|-|-|
0 1 2 3 4 5 6 7 8 9 10	0 1 2 3 4 5 6 7 8 9 10	0 1 2 3 4 5 6 7 8 9 10

Targeted

Stressful Thinking Level	Stressful Emotion Level	Stressful Symptom Level
|-|-|-|-|-|-|-|-|-|-|	|-|-|-|-|-|-|-|-|-|-|	|-|-|-|-|-|-|-|-|-|-|
0 1 2 3 4 5 6 7 8 9 10	0 1 2 3 4 5 6 7 8 9 10	0 1 2 3 4 5 6 7 8 9 10

Achieved

Stressful Thinking Level	Stressful Emotion Level	Stressful Symptom Level
|-|-|-|-|-|-|-|-|-|-|	|-|-|-|-|-|-|-|-|-|-|	|-|-|-|-|-|-|-|-|-|-|
0 1 2 3 4 5 6 7 8 9 10	0 1 2 3 4 5 6 7 8 9 10	0 1 2 3 4 5 6 7 8 9 10

Evaluation (What worked, what didn't?)

GROUP EXERCISE 11.2:
GROUP MENTAL REHEARSAL

In this exercise, the entire group selects a stress situation to work on. First, group members nominate situations. Then, members vote on which to use. The group then develops a 10-step hierarchy for the common situation, following the criteria discussed in this chapter. Once a hierarchy is agreed upon, a group mental rehearsal script is developed (including cues, irrational and self-defeating thinking, relaxation, rational and useful thinking and behavior, and completion thoughts). When developed, one group member (or the leader) leads the entire group in a mental rehearsal of this situation. At the end, the group discusses the strengths of the rehearsal and how it might be improved.

GROUP EXERCISE 11.3: STRESS HIERARCHY AND MENTAL REHEARSAL

(To be conducted by qualified mental health professional)

One group member volunteers to share a 10-situation stress path. Other members discuss the hierarchy, and whether each item is appropriately ranked.

The group member then describes the mental rehearsal cycle they have developed. Other members evaluate.

Exercises for Chapter 12

INDIVIDUAL EXERCISE 12.1:
COPING PHILOSOPHY

EXERCISE CONTRACT

I, _____, HEREBY
CONTRACT WITH MYSELF TO COMPLETE THE FOLLOWING
EXERCISE. IF I FINISH BY THE FOLLOWING DATE,
_____, I WILL GIVE MYSELF THIS REWARD:

SIGNATURE: _____ DATE: _____

In the space below, describe your coping philosophy. Incorporate
your thoughts about coping, defense, and relaxation.

Bibliography

Alberti, R. E. and Emmons, M. L. (1978). *Your perfect right: A guide to assertive behavior* (3d ed.). San Luis Obispo, CA: Impact Press.

Beck, A., Rush, J., Hollon, S., and Shaw, B. (1979). *Cognitive therapy of depression.* New York: Guildford.

Beecher, H. K. (1959). *Measurement of subjective responses.* New York: Oxford University Press.

Bower, S. A., and Bower, G. H. (1976). *Asserting yourself.* Melno Park, CA: Addison-Wesley.

Burns, D.D. (1989). *The feeling good handbook.* New York: William Morrow and Company.

Cannon, W. (1932). *The wisdom of the body.* New York: Norton.

D'Zurilla, T. J. (1986). *Problem-solving therapy: A social competence approach to clinical intervention.* New York: Springer Publishing Company.

Ellis, A. and Grieger, R. (Eds.). (1977). *Handbook of rational-emotive therapy.* New York: Springer.

Ellis, A. and Harper, R. A. (1975). *A new guide to rational living.* Englewood Cliffs, NJ: Prentice-Hall.

Goldstein, A. P. and Keller, H. R. (1987). *Aggressive behavior: Assessment and intervention.* New York: Pergamon.

Goldstein, A. P., Sprafkin, R. P., and Gershaw, N. J. (1976). *Skill training for community living.* New York: Pergamon.

Izard, C. E. (1977). *Human emotions.* New York: Plenum.

Jakubowski, P. and Lange, A. J. (1978). *Your perfect right.* Champaign, IL: Research Press.

Meichenbaum, D. (1985). *Stress inoculation training.* New York: Pergamon.

McMullin, R. E. (1986). *Handbook of cognitive therapy techniques.* New York: W. W. Norton.

Melzack, R. (1973). *The puzzle of pain.* New York: Basic Books.

Melzack, R. and Wall, P. D. (1965). Pain mechanisms: A new theory. *Science, 150,* 971-979.

Murphy, L. R. and Schoenborn, T. F. (Eds.). (1987). *Stress management in work settings.* (DHHA Publication No. 87-111). Washington, D.C.: U.S. Government Printing Office.

Schneider, C. J. (1987). Cost effectiveness of biofeedback and behavioral medicine treatments: A review of the literature. *Biofeedback and Self-Regulation, 12,* 71-92.

Smith, J. C. (1987). *Meditation: A sensible guide to a timeless discipline.* Champaign, IL: Research Press.

Smith, J. C. (1989). *Relaxation dynamics: A cognitive-behavioral approach to relaxation.* Champaign, IL: Research Press.

Smith, J. C. (1990). *Cognitive-behavioral relaxation training: A new system of strategies for treatment and assessment.* New York: Springer Publishing Company.

Smith, J. C. (in press). *The complete stress management book.* Englewood Cliffs, NJ: Prentice Hall.

Turk, D. C., Meichenbaum, D., and Genest, M. (1983). *Pain and behavioral medicine.* New York: The Guilford Press.

Index

About the Author

Jonathan C. Smith received his B.A. from Oberlin College and his Ph.D. in psychology from Michigan State University. He is currently a clinical psychologist, Associate Professor of Psychology at Roosevelt University in Chicago, and founder and Director of the Roosevelt University Stress Institute.

Dr. Smith's work on stress, relaxation, and meditation are well-known by both scientists and practitioners. His books include *Relaxation dynamics: A cognitive-behavioral approach to relaxation* (two editions), *Meditation: A sensible guide to a timeless discipline,* and *Cognitive-behavioral relaxation training: A new system of strategies for treatment and assessment.* He is currently completing two textbooks on stress management and a cognitive-behavioral guide to spiritual living. Dr. Smith's articles have appeared in the *Journal of Consulting and Clinical Psychology, American Psychologist, Psychological Bulletin, Biofeedback and Self-Regulation,* and *Perceptual and Motor Skills* and have been reprinted in a variety of major clinical textbooks.

Dr. Smith's work over the past decade has focused on developing a new system of relaxation based on cognitive-behavioral principles. His cognitive-behavioral relaxation training integrates progressive relaxation, yoga, breathing, self-hypnosis, imagery, autogenic training, contemplation, and meditation. In addition, it provides clear guidelines on how to teach, practice, and investigate relaxation.